What People Are Saying About

The Daimon and the Soul of the West

The Daimon and the Soul of the West packs quite a punch in its well-crafted text and I'm still reeling from its emotional impact. **Christof Koch, PhD**, author, neuroscientist, and former head of the Allen Institute for Brain Science

Gripping, insightful and highly instructive.
Patrick Harpur, author

Previous Books

*Rationalist Spirituality: An exploration of the meaning
of life and existence informed by logic and science*
Iff Books, ISBN: 978 1 84694 407 9

*Dreamed up Reality: Diving into mind to uncover
the astonishing hidden tale of nature*
Iff Books, ISBN: 978 1 84694 525 0

*Meaning in Absurdity: What bizarre phenomena can tell us
about the nature of reality*
Iff Books, ISBN: 978 1 84694 859 6

*Why Materialism Is Baloney: How true skeptics know there is no
death and fathom answers to life, the universe, and everything*
Iff Books, ISBN: 978 1 78279 362 5

*Brief Peeks Beyond: Critical essays on metaphysics,
neuroscience, free will, skepticism and culture*
Iff Books, ISBN: 978 1 78535 018 4

More Than Allegory: On religious myth, truth and belief
Iff Books, ISBN: 978 1 78535 287 4

*The Idea of the World: A multi-disciplinary argument
for the mental nature of reality*
Iff Books, ISBN: 978 1 78535 739 8

*Decoding Schopenhauer's Metaphysics: The key to understanding
how it solves the hard problem of consciousness
and the paradoxes of quantum mechanics*
Iff Books, ISBN: 978 1 78904 426 3

*Decoding Jung's Metaphysics: The archetypal semantics
of an experiential universe*
Iff Books, ISBN: 978 1 78904 565 9

*Science Ideated: The fall of matter and the contours
of the next mainstream scientific worldview*
Iff Books, ISBN: 978 1 78904 668 7

*Analytic Idealism in a Nutshell: A straightforward summary
of the 21st-century's only plausible metaphysics*
Iff Books, ISBN: 978 1 80341 669 4

The Daimon and
the Soul of the West

Bernardo Kastrup

The Daimon and

the Soul of the West

Bernardo Kastrup

IFF BOOKS

London, UK
Washington, DC, USA

CollectiveInk

First published by iff Books, 2025
iff Books is an imprint of Collective Ink Ltd.,
Unit 11, Shepperton House, 89 Shepperton Road, London, N1 3DF
office@collectiveinkbooks.com
www.collectiveinkbooks.com
www.iff-books.com

For distributor details and how to order please visit the 'Ordering' section on our website.

Text copyright: Bernardo Kastrup 2024

ISBN: 978 1 80341 949 7 (Paperback)
978 1 80341 950 3 (ebook)
Library of Congress Control Number: 2024945146

A CIP catalogue record for this book is available from the British Library.

Design: Lapiz Digital Services

UK: Printed and bound by CPI Group (UK) Ltd, Croydon, CR0 4YY
Printed in North America by CPI GPS partners

We operate a distinctive and ethical publishing philosophy in all areas of our business, from our global network of authors to production and worldwide distribution.

Contents

Contents

To Claudia, the rock upon which my life and work stand.

Und mich ergreift ein längst entwöhntes Sehnen
Nach jenem stillen ernsten Geisterreich,
Es schwebet nun in unbestimmten Tönen
Mein lispelnd Lied, der Äolsharfe gleich,
Ein Schauer faßt mich, Thräne folgt den Thränen,
Das strenge Herz es fühlt sich mild und weich;
Was ich besitze seh' ich wie im Weiten,
Und was verschwand wird mir zu Wirklichkeiten.

And I am seized by a long-lost yearning
For that quiet, earnest realm of ghosts,
It now floats in indefinite tones,
My whispering song, like the Aeolian harp,
A shudder seizes me, tears follow tears,
The stern heart feels mild and soft;
What I possess I see as if in the distance,
And what is gone becomes reality to me.

Johann Wolfgang von Goethe
(English translation by the author)

Chapter 1

Setting Sail from Ogygia

This book is the inevitable outcome, in me, of a simple but momentous realization: we, Western minds, have forgotten who we are, despite having never once stopped being who we are. We've lost touch with the primordial impetus that fuels the inner fire of our vitality, as well as the innate, archetypal dispositions we embody. We've forgotten the inner chamber in the palace of mind where we stem from, as well as why we came into being and what we're supposed to do. No longer can we sense the immanent context that couches our lives in purpose, or the ever-present inner compass without which we can't navigate life adequately. We've lost our sense of identity and, therefore, that of family and belonging. In the throes of disorientation and emptiness, we've even come to deny the very notions of natural identity, inherent purpose, and objective meaning: we've come to deny our natural selves, believing instead that the self is an arbitrary construct that we are free to reinvent, tweak, and otherwise force to comply with convenience and escapist strategies. There is nothing inherent, natural, inescapable about us—or so we think. Instead, we are *tabula rasa*—blank slates— to be filled by the whims, accidents, and circumstances of life. Indeed, we've drifted so far from home we've forgotten even that there is such a place as home, and such a way of life as rootedness in eternity.

Our amnesia has created a huge empty space in the core of our being, a hollow in the middle of our chest. Like a blackhole, it has its own irresistible gravity well; like a vacuum, it sucks things in, demands to be filled. And so, we dutifully—even obsequiously—attempt to fill it with made-up narratives, projections, and artificial, culture-bound recipes. We tell ourselves that we can be whoever we like to be; that we can not only do as we want, but—absurdly—want as we want. Masters of the self we are—or so we want to believe. We proclaim that life is what we make of it, that the world means what we make it mean. This Promethean attitude is as understandable as it is hopeless, as endearing as it is unnatural. For it simply *doesn't work*, does it? It never did, and it never will. After all, we are entities produced by nature and rooted in reality, not characters in a capricious autobiographical fantasy. We won't stop being what we are just because we tell ourselves convenient stories. This is so obvious it is embarrassing to have to affirm it. We won't find solace in our escapist fantasies, for solace is the result of an alignment—a resonance—between our inner attitude and our true nature. And to find that resonance we must first remember, and then acknowledge, *reality*: the reality of our own being and that of the world from which we emerge.

Our forgetting our inborn nature and role has led to a tragic schism in our collective psyche: a divorce between nature and narrative, being and action. This book is an effort to help heal that schism. It is about re-encountering ourselves, remembering how to live naturally; about recalling the archetypal templates and dispositions we embody, what we stand for, and how to navigate the choppy waters of life so to re-align ourselves with the inherent, objective meaning of our ephemeral existences. Its journey represents a return to origins and identity, to authenticity, clarity, and instinctive vitality; a return to the spontaneity of being at home, where the natural energies that kindle our inner fire are allowed to flow.

Contrary to our usual escapism, this return home is a confrontation with reality, not convenient narratives. And there is much about reality that doesn't fit our tastes and fancies. But that's okay, for our life isn't—has never been, will never be—about our personal satisfaction, happiness, or bucket list. What nature is trying to do through you and me is about *nature*, not you or me. Insofar as my own experience is representative of general truths, there is no viable alternative to living according to nature, *our* nature. Such is the spirit of this book.

Unlike my previous works, this isn't a book with an argument. I cannot even hope to objectively defend its message through logic or measurable evidence, for it belongs in the realm of inner life, of soul existence. As such, I can only hope to convey my message to you by striving to help you recognize it *in yourself*. It is this *recognition* that renders objective arguments redundant. For when we see in ourselves that which we are, we know it *by direct acquaintance* and no longer need conceptual abstractions that merely point to it. When we see what the pointing finger is indicating, we no longer need the pointing finger. By *remembering* something ever present in you, I hope you won't need a story—a compelling argument—from me. For the reality of what you will then remember resonates within us *as* us, not as a message addressed *to* us.

Yet, how can a book, which by its very nature demands that you orient your attention outwards, help you recognize that which resides in yourself? Well, perhaps by analogy with someone else's inner life, inner reality; someone who shares with you the burden of being human. And that someone I can indeed hope to be. All I can thus do is lay my humanity bare in front of you, in all its fullness and vulnerability. For this humanity is what I have in common with you. Perhaps through the history of my own inner life I can help you evoke in yourself that which I hope you will recognize. For this reason, this book has many autobiographical elements, even though it is far from being an autobiography. My hope is that, by sharing my own raw humanity with you, I can place in front of you a mirror that will help you discern my intended meaning. I hope you will recognize in me that which lives in you, too.

But what is this "Westerness" that this book talks about? Who belongs in this group, and who decides who is in or out?

Westerness is not a location. In fact, today its correlation with the geographical west is merely incidental, a throwback to historical contingencies that are no longer relevant. I have seen more compelling Westerness in Japan and South Korea than in some places in the Americas—and that's not even to mention Australia and New Zealand. Once upon a time, what I call "the West" was indeed much more prevalent west of the Bosphorus Strait than east, and so the label "West" stuck; that's all. In this book, I persist in the use of the term simply because it is the most colloquially recognizable.

Neither is the West a race or ethnicity. As a matter of fact, the scientific case for modern humans having races is precarious at best. Dogs do have races: any two Pugs will look more like each other than any one of them will look like any Great Dane. In dogs, groups have internally consistent and externally distinguishable characteristics. Humans don't. People we refer to as "Blacks," "Whites," "Asians," etc., all exhibit the full range of heights, weights, facial and bodily proportions, mental dispositions and skills, etc. I believe no reasonable person will deny that I have more physically in common with many East Africans than I have with, say, Danny DeVito. I share with East Africans my height and some elongated skeletal features, while DeVito has rounder, stockier features. Yet, those who believe in the existence of human races will almost certainly rather group me with DeVito than East Africans. So, no, the West is not about races, for modern humans have no such thing. Those who think we do simply have a peculiar form of selective attention: they only see *some* literally superficial features—such as skin color—and fail to notice all the rest.

Humans admittedly do have genealogies, because any member of a sexually reproducing species has a genealogy—i.e., a genetic or family history, a pedigree. But psychological dispositions such as those I associate with the West, even if they are genetic at root, aren't consistent within lineages. Just think of how different children can be from their parents when it comes to their personalities, tastes, wants, priorities, values, etc. Moreover, economic integration and low-cost, fast transportation technologies have largely globalized the human population. The geographical isolation and inbreeding of lineages that originally led to what we call human ethnicities is in decline, and thus cannot account for what I mean by "Westerness," which is very alive and growing.

Westerness is a set of innate values and an instinctive inclination to a certain way of life, an inherent mindset, an inborn mode of being and expressing oneself in the world. The Western mind embodies a particular and recognizable set of psychological archetypes— primordial templates of thinking, feeling, wanting, and behaving—and associated dispositions. As such, the West is a psychosocial grouping, not a geographical or ethnic one, this being its strength and the basis of its long-term viability.

As a philosopher, I have the tendency to look to history for metaphors and representative examples of what I am trying to express. But though this might make me sound erudite, it is also less relatable—more remote, abstract—than examples from contemporary culture. And as it happens, there is a near-perfect metaphorical example, in twenty-first-century popular culture, of what I mean by a set of values and way of life that define a group. Just think of the *Jedi* in the *Star Wars* fantasy universe: there are Jedi from multiple species, coming from multiple planets and star systems in that galaxy far away. Not only are races irrelevant to being Jedi, but even species and entire trees of life as well. Geography also means nothing, as the Jedi stem from all corners of the galaxy. What unifies them—what makes them *Jedi*—is *a set of values and a way of life*, modes of being and relating to self, each other, others, and the world. The West is something like that: we aren't unified by ethnicities or geography, but by how we express ourselves in the world. The latter, in turn, is determined by the archetypal dispositions we embody. An attempt to reveal the archetypes and dispositions that define the Western mind is the journey of the chapters that follow.

Before we start, however, a couple of observations are prudent, as I attempt to anticipate and prevent pernicious misunderstandings of the above from snowballing. I do think the archetypal dispositions we embody and express are inborn, not merely learned. Yet, I also think that they aren't meaningfully correlated with so-called ethnicities. Whatever genetic factors might play a role in their genesis seem to be distributed throughout humanity—among "Blacks," "Whites," "Asians," etc.—and not confined to particular ethnic groups. For example, in the early twenty-first century there are few media voices more unambiguously and uncompromisingly Western than Fareed Zakaria's, an Indian from Mumbai, born in a Konkani Muslim family. So my claim of inborn factors should not be mistaken for an endorsement of "racial theory" in any way or form.

My calling for the recognition of our identity as Westerners also does *not* entail or imply a ranking of minds or cultures. That I believe in such a thing as the Western mind does *not* mean that I consider it inherently superior—or inferior—to others. Doing so would be akin to claiming that the yellow pigment in Vincent van Gogh's *The Starry Night* is better than the blue one. The claim would be absurd, as the different pigments only have the majestic effect they have when they complement and contrast with each other. In this same spirit, it is abundantly clear to me that the human journey can only exhaust its potential through the interplay of distinct ways of being and living. As I'll discuss in more detail later, all my life I have been an overt admirer of non-Western cultures. They have enriched me, expanded my horizons, provided depth and nuance to my understanding of self and world, none of which would have been possible without the contrasts they offered to my own dispositions. The spirit of this book is thus not just the recognition of identity, but also the celebration of diversity. I say this not to signal my virtues in the confused age of woke, but because it is self-evident to me.

Finally, it is important to acknowledge upfront that no social group is purely Western, just as no social group lacks Westerness completely. Nature doesn't deal in binaries. Nobody owns Westerness and nobody is defined exclusively by it. We all express a multitude of archetypal dispositions, a rainbow of values and modes of thinking, feeling, wanting, and behaving. So when I speak of Western minds, what I am really talking about is *mostly* Western minds; minds in which the values and ways of being that define Westerness are more prominent than other values and ways of being. There are no purely Western countries, just as there are no purely Eastern countries. Easterness and Westerness are ingredients in the complex recipes that give rise to our minds and hearts. Yet, they are distinct, identifiable ingredients.

With these clarifications in place, let us now start our journey towards the rediscovery of ourselves and the hidden templates that govern our lives.

Chapter 2
The Cyclops's Cave of Mysteries

I was born in 1974, the year in which two seminal events occurred that would set the tone for my entire life. The first was Thomas Nagel's publication of his paper, "What is it like to be a bat?" Nagel's work brought phenomenal consciousness—the qualities of experience—back into the investigative agenda in Western academia, after the dark, grotesque decades of Logical Positivism and Behaviorism. It started a process in Western culture that would eventually pull me in and set the context for my work as a philosopher. The second seminal event was Federico Faggin's creation of the Z80 microprocessor at Zilog, which would go on to become one of the key enablers of the home microcomputer revolution and motivate me to pursue computer engineering 17 years later. Looking back, it's funny to see how my paths in life seemed to be prefigured already at my birth.

Because of the microcomputer revolution started largely by Faggin, my generation was the first to be able to express their imagination in the worlds of computer games and bedroom coding. You would think that this meant a lot of time spent indoors, and sure enough it did. But there was also another, very different side to my childhood, which not many of my peers had the privilege to experience.

I grew up in Rio de Janeiro, Brazil. Although one of the most densely populated and heavily urbanized places in the world, Rio was—and I trust still is, despite my not having been there in almost three decades—surrounded by the Atlantic Forest. About 50 Km (30 miles) out of town, my maternal grandfather owned a country property, which the family used for weekend gatherings. It encompassed a hill—with the main house perched right on top of it—and most of the west side of a small mountain. The latter was blanketed by dense, dark green, luxuriant Atlantic Forest canopy. That property is one of my fondest childhood memories, an idyllic place filled with the magic of colorful birds, noisy insects, trees and fruits more varied than my child mind could hope to catalogue, and... mystery; uncanny, morally ambiguous, pulsating mystery.

The front yard of the main house had a small swimming pool where my cousins and I would spend much of our time. From the pool, looking towards the east, the mountain—whose foot was some 400m or a quarter of a mile away from the house—looked imposing, like a very old, primordial creature whose movements were just too slow and labored for us to perceive. To see the peak, we had to literally tilt our heads backwards a little, due to its proximity and fast-rising slopes. Indeed, seen through my child-eyes, that mountain—quite small for Swiss standards, which would come to reset my references only a few years later—was a majestic giant, commanding awe, respect, and admiration. And unlike Swiss mountains, the giant was geologically ancient, very ancient, featuring no loose rocks or jagged edges. Instead, it radiated smooth, granitoid solidity, invulnerability, and gravitas. So powerful it was, in fact, that it could easily crush—without even noticing—these puny, mayfly-like little creatures at its foot, weren't it too slow to move in time to catch us.

About two-thirds of the way to the top, a lone rocky outcrop jutted out of the forest canopy; a small—but very conspicuous— point where the giant was naked; a seeming vulnerability in the armor of the otherwise indomitable titan. The top half of the outcrop had a protruding ledge or overhang—like a thick eyelid—hiding a small speck of darkness just below and behind it. That was the giant's single eye, and I was sure it hid the entrance to a cave wherein mysteries lay undiscovered. Looking fixedly at the outcrop from the pool, I wondered endlessly about what those might be. Nothing feeds the imagination of a child more than a mystery; it dissolves the banality of life like acid.

Thinking back to it today, I am not sure there ever was any cave at all. The outcrop's "eyelid" simply projected a little shadow underneath it, which produced the illusion of some sort of hidden entrance. As a child, however, this thought not once occurred to me. I *knew* it was the entrance to a hidden cave; that was obvious. And it instigated in me an irresistible urge to explore, despite the uncanniness and utter moral ambiguity of what I intuited might be found inside. The naked outcrop— the exposed eye of the giant—was like a siren song. It seduced and attracted sailors to the deep within, and possibly to their deaths. Once inside—I fantasized—one may never be able to come out again. How exciting!

I mounted countless expeditions up the mountain to find the entrance to the cave. Sometimes I would go accompanied by a cousin or friends, but more often than not I would climb up alone and go higher and deeper into the forest than when accompanied. Because the west side of the mountain was part of my grandfather's property, my family had a naïve sense of safety: nothing could happen to me if I remained within the boundaries of their own place, right? Little did they know. They never had any idea that I was trying to get to that rocky outcrop so high up; they had no clue how narrow and slippery the trail was, and how steep its slopes. And it was better that way.

But I wasn't careless or overconfident. Even as a child, I knew better; better than my parents, in any case. And so there was always thorough preparation involved: suitable protective clothing and shoes, a backpack filled with food, water, knifes, ropes, binoculars, etc., and a high-pressure air riffle for good measure (my father had taught me to use that thing when I was eight or nine years old). After all, one may have to defend oneself against the uncanny threats hidden in the cave, not to mention the multitude of very real reptiles hiding along the edges of the trail. If I were to wear a bandana, I might have looked like a small version of Mr. Rambo himself, ready for combat and survival challenges. But I was well past this kind of silliness: confronting the mystery was very real and very serious business indeed; I knew it in the core of my being.

The initial part of the trail, starting at the foot of the giant, meandered through grassy terrain with bushes and shrubs, brightly lit by the relentless tropical sun. Patches of bare, iron oxide-rich red soil scarred it here and there, like burn marks. From this area, one could see as far as the Atlantic shore to the south, as well as a huge brackish water lagoon to the west. One felt like rising slowly above the everyday world, where banality seemed to prevail, and towards a boundary, a liminal region that separated everyday reality from another, different kind of reality.

The transition, when it came, was abrupt: in a few short steps, one would leave the clear, sunlit world of the dry, grassy terrain and enter an impossibly dark, humid region where the forest canopy was so dense that precious little light penetrated it. The trail suddenly narrowed to something hardly broader than my shoulders, odd pieces of vegetation stubbornly refusing to obey the boundary lines humans like to project onto nature. Now and then, a fallen tree—victim of Thor's latest fits of rage—would block the way, being defeated only by the kind of bodily acrobatics kids can muster. The incessant chorus of bird and insect chanting almost overwhelmed the ears, its sources obviously near but nonetheless elusive. It felt like being gripped by hands one couldn't see. The feeling of being constantly stared at—even scrutinized—by a thousand invisible, nonhuman eyes was palpable.

The deeper one would go in, the narrower the trail and the darker the atmosphere would become. At a certain point, one's will to face the mystery would be tested to the limit: the trail cut across the moist and mossy bed of what, in a rainy day, would surely be the middle height of a waterfall. This was the narrowest and most dangerous crossing, the only one where little in the way of vegetation would arrest one's fall if one were to slip. Loose pieces of rock, eroded to a very smooth texture and covered in moss, were the only things one could step on. Playing these memories back as an adult, it surprises me how insanely dangerous it was for a kid to even attempt the crossing. Yet, I did it more times than I could count, almost hugging the side of the mountain with my arms outstretched, as I tested the firmness of every rock before taking the next step.

Eventually the trail would come to a complete end, only a daunting, dense, and intricate tangle of branches, vines, and shrubs being left to negotiate in the surreal darkness of the forest. Right at that point lay a particularly large and smooth boulder, which kind of invited you to sit on it. Its shape was almost ergonomic—peculiar happenstance given that, at that point of the climb, one would be tired and in need of a clear, solid place to sit on for a while.

What happened next was repeated every single time I made the attempt to reach the cave. I would sit on my "sofa boulder," as I called it, and lay my backpack, air rifle and machete next to me. While munching on my sandwich and sipping my refreshments, I would then peek through the dark tangle of vegetation ahead, discerning what appeared to be a bright, sunlit clearing some 40 or 50 meters (yards) ahead. That *must* have been the rocky outcrop—with the entrance to the cave and its mysteries—lying just ahead, as there were no other places uncovered by tree canopy on the west side of the mountain. I *knew* it was the cave, tantalizingly close, reachable through vegetation that my machete would have made short work of in some 15 minutes, tops. That mysterious and enchanting place, which called me like an irresistibly seductive mistress, lay within my grasp. I had all but arrived at long last.

Then, I would pack all my stuff again, stand up decidedly, and... turn around and go back down.

Again and again, weekend after weekend, after much planning and preparation, I would brave my perilous way to the sofa boulder, have a refreshment, contemplate my goal—a symbol of the ultimate purpose of my childhood—lying right ahead, within easy reach, and then turn around and go back as if that were the only logical course of action. I experienced no cognitive dissonance, no inner struggle, not even a hint of doubt or befuddlement. Having just spent a whole afternoon single-mindedly pursuing my childhood dream, I *knew* the self-evident next step—*the only possible step*—was to return home just before realizing it.

As an adult, I spent a lot of time thinking about this odd but consistent peculiarity of my child-self. The conclusion of years of meditation on this is what this book is about: the labored insights of a deeply Western mind systematically surprised by itself, disappointed in itself, wrestling with itself, deceiving and defeating itself in a frantic attempt to understand and accept itself.

The non-existing cave of my childhood was a *symbol* of something very real and present in the Western mind: the urge to confront and ponder a certain profound mystery; the overpowering drive to realize an archetypal goal so deep it can't even be thought. This fundamental template of the Western mind expressed itself almost overwhelmingly in my child-self. It projected its own urges onto the world around me, thereby creating the felt reality of a cave of mysteries just beyond my reach. That living symbol indelibly marked my childhood and drew the map of my entire life. Climbing the giant was a metaphorical rehearsal for the coming twists and turns of my fate.

Indeed, the quest for the magic cave was the first and most memorable expression of the teleological drive that underlies my life. The Greek word *telos* (τέλος) is ordinarily translated as goal or purpose. But I will use it in this book in the sense not of an ordinary purpose, but a *transcendent* one; i.e., a goal beyond conceptual logic, which cannot be corralled into mere words or understood in merely rational terms; an eternal goal that can only be projected onto the canvas of our lives in a seemingly ambiguous, precarious, symbolic manner, and yet can be very concretely felt in the core of our being as something irresistibly powerful.

Teleological drive is one of the basic archetypes of the Western mind. It commands us to live for a purpose, even though a purpose we can't quite grasp or make sense of. It demands that we orient our lives towards the cave where unfathomable mysteries lie hidden from direct sight, and which is accessible only through a small vulnerability in the armor of the monstruous universe surrounding us; a small, naked outcrop jutting out of the otherwise impenetrable canopy of mystery. The Western mind is the one most prone to being seduced by the siren song of the uncanny; it is, in fact, perhaps the one that *hears* the siren song most clearly. How could one be surprised that science was born in the West?

Paradoxically, however, our secret fear of realizing the goal—of fulfilling the telos—is so overwhelming that we erect many lines of defense against it. The first of these lines is very recognizable today: we deny that any telos at all is interwoven with the fabric of nature. We (want to) believe, instead, that whatever purpose life may have is one defined by ourselves, subjectively, not something objective or given. And by convincing ourselves rationally that life has no intrinsic purpose, we release ourselves from any uncomfortable feeling of responsibility or duty. There's nothing we need to do, no transcendent call we need to heed, for nature is fundamentally stupid; it expects nothing of us for it has no purpose—or so the story goes. As a result, we can relax and focus all our energies egotistically *on ourselves*, on our *personal* agendas, on the attempt to be happy, as opposed to being of service to something beyond ourselves. Ironically, this is precisely the reason why many of us are *un*happy: a life without a natural, objective telos is a life without meaning. Whatever personal, subjective goal we set for ourselves is immediately recognized in the root of our being as artificial, manufactured, a form of self-deception, even if we don't rationally acknowledge it.

The second line of defense against our natural telos is to stop just short of seriously setting out to achieve it, just as my child-self stopped just short of the final straight towards the entrance of the cave of mysteries. We have a deep, archetypal fear of being disappointed or of having to face something uncanny and disturbing. We intuitively smell that something fundamental about the world and ourselves may not be to our liking; may not fit with our expectations; may exceed our categories and ability to comprehend and integrate. Therefore, we stop within sight of the destination. Although we have the means to cut through the final 40 or 50 meters of vegetation, the sunlight piercing through the dark canopy right ahead is a harbinger of the eerie; it petrifies us. We rather turn around and go back, lest we find ghastly things inside or—the mother of all catastrophes—discover that *there has never been a cave at all*; at least not in the sense we had imagined there should be. We can withstand great pain and suffering, but we can't bear realizing that the arduous journey was for no reason; at least in the sense we thought it should have a reason. Thus, we prefer to manufacture our own goals—which exist in the sense we expect them to, even if they are self-made deceptions—rather than wasting our lives pursuing what we might eventually conclude to be a mirage.

Fear of the dark cave of secrets is the flipside of the telos archetype, and as integral to it as the urge to fulfill the telos itself. Every archetype has its shadow, its dark side, and teleology is no exception. The same siren song that pulls us in also repulses us. We are terrified of what we most wish to have; of what we absolutely *need* to have. The opposite of love is not hate but fear. And so, we both irresistibly love and irresistibly fear what nature demands to discover through us. The love and the fear are the two sides of one coin.

Throughout my childhood I experienced, embodied, and gave expression to the telos archetype in myriad different ways. I always had a "project," which set a direction for, and motivated, my thoughts, feelings, and actions for a certain period of time, until it would be replaced by some other project. Myriad projects came and went, from programming games on my home computer, to finding out how to spawn some rare fish in my aquarium, to building spaceships (fantasy spaceships, you'd say, but for me they were prototypes of the real thing to come), to contacting aliens by hacking into my father's HAM radio equipment.

Some might say that my child-self was never "in the moment," since he was always focused on some purpose or goal, as opposed to what was immediately in front of him. But I beg to differ: my child-self was indeed in the moment, *precisely by virtue of having a goal*. For him, it was the context provided by the goal that invested the moment with importance, significance, vibrancy, and aliveness. The moment was only substantial insofar as it served a telos; short of it, it was ephemeral and insignificant—it was, well, *for nothing*.

This is how the telos archetype rehearsed its expression in my child-self, before taking the reins of my adult life. My childhood projects were training for what was to come. They helped me get used to a certain template of thinking, feeling, wanting, and acting—a particular way of being in the world—so I could later serve nature's telos. Yet, before that time of service began in earnest, a long interlude of disillusionment would come to dominate my life...

Chapter 3

The *Axis Mundi*

Throughout my childhood, my father would—laughingly but regularly—claim that he had "blue blood." At first, as a preschooler, I figured that this had to do with blood determining the color of one's eyes. My father had blue eyes, so his blood must have been blue, I thought. Alas, as impeccable as my logic was, it turns out that the blue blood thing was an allusion to his being related to the Danish royal family (my father's family had a Danish immigrant background). Although he would invariably make the claim tongue-in-cheek, he would also repeat it so consistently that, to my child-mind, it must have been factual. As a matter of fact, even his HAM radio station was called "station blue blood," an identifier he proudly broadcasted to the world—in multiple languages—each night in the wee hours. It couldn't have been just a joke, I reasoned.

Years later, after my father's passing, I asked my paternal grandmother about our royal relations. She burst into a heart-felt belly laugh—an impossibly rare thing for her, after the loss of both of her adult children—and told me: "our family emigrated because we were dirt-poor!" So much for my royal heritage.

Relieved as I was with not having to live up to regal standards, my father's recurring joke—as well as less implausible claims of aristocratic heritage on my mother's, Portuguese side of the family—nonetheless triggered a formative realization in my mind: we are not born in a vacuum, without a history or a context; instead, we are the latest in an unspeakably long line of unfathomable human drama, of epic stories, love affairs and heartbreaks, great adventures and migrations, achievements and misfortunes, great losses and conquests, insights and regrets.

Countless previous generations live in each one of us. Our ancestors—whether genetically related to us or not—look at the world through our eyes. The dead are alive in us. They expect us to live their unlived lives, achieve their unattained goals, complete their unfinished work, turn over the rocks they couldn't turn, so together we can realize our common purpose. They expect us to vindicate them and give meaning to their existence, just as we strive to give meaning to our own. As we go about our lives, we carry a crowd of the dead along with us, peering over our shoulders. For we are each the tip of an arrow that spans the eons, pages in the middle of an epic book whose continuation depends on the words we write through our actions and inactions. A momentous day it is when, at some point in our development, we become aware of this reality. Friedrich Nietzsche spoke of it thus:

> When we dream of persons long forgotten or dead, it is a sign that we have suffered radical changes, and that the soil on which we live has been completely undermined. *The dead rise again, and our antiquity becomes modernity.*
> (*Writings of Nietzsche: Volume III*, edited by Anthony Uyl, Devoted Publishing, 2017, page 150, my emphasis)

As I turn 50 and my maturity finally dawns and begins to illuminate the remainder of my path, I have a calm, self-assured sense that Bernardo Kastrup is but one face—even a mere façade—of an ageless collective. So many lives are lived in me, and through me. Carl Gustav Jung, Arthur Schopenhauer—whose legacies I have written about in earlier books—and countless anonymous others, who have labored and suffered through the ages, stand behind me and look over my shoulders as my own self continues to unfold with every step I take.

The felt presence of the ancestors can be so concrete as to hijack our emotional inner lives. After I became acquainted with Schopenhauer's work, for instance, I felt an irresistible urge to vindicate the man. For his ideas were so far ahead of his time—even of my own time—that he has been systematically misinterpreted and misrepresented by ostensible academic authorities who should know better. To my own astonishment, I felt the frustration and outrage I'd only expect to feel if it had been my own work that was so disgracefully defaced. I lived what I imagine would have been Schopenhauer's inner turmoil had he been here to witness what was done to his legacy. And with this feeling came an overwhelming sense of responsibility for defending the man, repairing the damage done to his work, and achieving at least some degree of justice and closure in his name. This is the power of the ancestors who live in us, and through us: *we feel their feelings*.

The archetypal templates embodied by our spiritual predecessors return in our own lives, sometimes in curiously specific ways. For instance, like Benedictus de Spinoza, I also have an Iberian background and found my spiritual home in the Netherlands. Like him, I am a philosopher who ponders the deeper nature of mind and reality, arguing his case based on objective reasoning, not spiritual insight. Like him, I speak Dutch in daily life, though my mother tongue—just as his—is Portuguese. Like his work, mine is also written in the main academic language of its time—English in the case of my books, Latin in the case of his. Like him, I am considered a heretic by the mainstream thinking of my era. Like him, I did philosophy while earning my living with high technology—namely, developing electronics enabled by lithographic lenses, while Spinoza grinded and polished lenses for microscopes and telescopes. Finally, like his, my commitment to my fate did not leave space for children—our books are our "children." We are all fractal reflections of our ancestors, and they of theirs, all the way back to the primordial beginning. The templates of their very being reside in us, for we are all expressions of the same underlying reality.

The felt presence of the ancestors, though occasionally oppressive, is invariably reassuring, sometimes consoling, and always provide felt depth and meaning to my existence. For my journey is but the tip of a transpersonal arrow shot at the dawn of the genus *Homo* itself. Whether I understand where this arrow comes from, where it is headed, what it is made of, and who shot it, is entirely beside the point; indeed, it is as irrelevant as whether the apple blossom knows what its role in the greater scheme of apple trees is. All that matters is my awareness of this arrow and my deliberate willingness to play my part in giving its flight continuation. For it is this awareness that vanquishes—with the ease with which turning on a light vanquishes darkness—the demons of meaninglessness and aloneness. I am never alone. I see countless faces in the mirror, many of which are ancient, remote, even pre-human. And not even my inaction is devoid of a point—of a purpose, a telos—let alone my countless failures.

Our entire lives are couched in unfathomable historical context, in the unfolding of a cosmic drama of which, in the present act, we are the protagonists. The origins of our stories recede far behind the mists of pre-history, into primordial time. And these stories shall continue—long after us—towards a teleological future as unfathomable to us as our own world would have been unfathomable to Schopenhauer, Parmenides, *Homo habilis*, and the first unicellular organism. Dazzled and overwhelmed by the monstrous immensity of this context, we now carry the baton. It is our turn in the race, whether we like it or not, for the dead can only live through us. And thirsty for life they are.

The sheer vastness of the context in which we are born links us to the entire dance of existence—to the central axis of the world, the mythological *Axis Mundi*—not just our genetic ancestors. Would my father's family have emigrated from Denmark if the 1864 Schleswig War with Prussia—which exacerbated poverty in my ancestral land well into the twentieth century—hadn't taken place? Could Otto von Bismarck's decision to start that war have been subtly inspired by Richard Wagner's triumphant operas? Given what we know today, this isn't implausible. And if so, could Wagner owe some of his own inspiration to Schopenhauer's idealist philosophy, of which we know he was an avid reader? In this case, my very physical existence as Bernardo Kastrup could be traced back to a seminal touch of Schopenhauer's pen to a sheet of paper, before 1818. My existence may be the continuation of a seminal thought in Schopenhauer's mind. Without the latter, Bernardo Kastrup might have never come to be. (None of this should be interpreted as my celebrating the 1864 Schleswig War. I don't. That war was a catastrophe for my ancestors, and no war of choice has my sympathy. The above is simply a factual acknowledgment that my existence—just as everyone else's—is a product of the twists and turns of history, whether they are morally appropriate or not. And neither do I blame the works of Schopenhauer or Wagner for the—unfortunate, unjustified— cognitive associations they've become entangled with in the minds of others.)

Analogously to the above, countless other links—involving perhaps less famous but equally important characters—could plausibly be conceived between my very existence and the unfathomable vastness of the past. I, as an individual, am connected back to the entirety of humanity's passion before me, and forward to its entire future unfolding. I am a page in humanity's epic, and so are you. It is the context provided by the pages that precede and succeed ours that couch our lives in *meaning*; meaning so vast it is impossible for any human to fully fathom.

For the meaning of our lives cannot be grasped without full context. If you were to pluck a random page from Homer's *The Odyssey*, in and of itself it would mean nothing. But in their context, each page is a necessary link that makes the story whole and meaningful. Read them all in the correct sequence, and the symbolic meaning of *The Odyssey* — both literally and figuratively, in the sense of the *telos* of the odyssey — comes alive in all its radiance and glory.

What creates space for depression and ennui is our failure to appreciate that, only within a context that far transcends our ability to grasp, does the meaning of our lives reveal itself. As such, this meaning is quite literally transcendent. Yet we can sense its presence — feel its scent, hear its music — through the myriad links that have brought the epic of human existence to the seminal moment of our birth. And only we can give continuity to this epic, even though we will never be able to anticipate or grasp its ultimate destination.

The Western mind, even in the throes of banality and nihilism, knows this instinctively. This is why we are so interested in the details of history, the dates of battles and the names of kings, as well as our own family's stories and genealogy. The popularity of historical dramas in Western media and literature reflects this archetypal disposition of the Western mind. We intuitively sense that the entrance to the palace of meaning can only be found across the vast fields of history, even if we can't articulate it to ourselves. Only past and future can lift our lives off the flats of banality and up epic mountains, turning our stories into tales of heroism and significance. All we need to do is to contemplate our stories *in context*.

Indeed, the past is corrosive to banality. Choices and events that feel meaningless and random in the present moment start to gain an aura of significance as they drift into the past, for their context becomes thicker and their consequences more developed.

Once, casually strolling down a corridor at my University in late 1993, I chanced upon a small announcement affixed to a wall. It was about a research program for undergraduate students, which was part of a collaboration with CERN, the European Organization for Nuclear Research. That corridor was in an obscure corner of the institute of physics, a building far away from the engineering school where I attended classes. I didn't need to be there, so my chancing upon the poster could easily have never happened. In fact, there's a sense in which it shouldn't have; it was a banal coincidence. But because it did happen, my life took a transformative turn away from the direction in which it had been pointing up until then.

As that "coincidental" moment drifted further into the past, its banality transmuted into one of the most significant plot twists of my story, largely determining the character of my contribution to humanity's telos. For CERN would become my first employer and the physics done there my first true, deep scientific love. Working there not only predisposed me to the strong empirical grounding that would come to characterize my later philosophical work, but it also provided the context that triggered its development: it was because of their applications to nuclear physics that I first worked on artificial neural networks. This, in turn, forced me to ask the questions about artificial sentience that led to the development of Analytic Idealism, the philosophy I am mostly known for.

Although the example above is a particularly compelling one, one must wonder to what degree the same applies to other, less conspicuous moments. Maybe you met the love of your life because one day you serendipitously decided to enter a shop, even though you didn't really need to buy anything. Maybe a casual conversation with a stranger led you to a job transition that defined the rest of your career. Had Alexander "the Great" chosen not to have that last, fateful drink in 330 BC, he might not have burned down Persepolis. Had Rudolf Diesel been awakened by a trigger-happy rooster earlier than usual in that fateful morning in 1893, he might not have had the dream that led him to the diesel engine. History—all of history—is determined by seeming banality.

Indeed, what we call banality is often merely an illusion of the *present*; an artifact of the immediacy of the moment, which causes a kind of cognitive myopia or shortsightedness. The felt presence of the moment is obfuscating; it shrinks our cognitive pupil, reduces our field of view, and prevents an apprehension of the objective meaning and significance inherent to existence. The reality of all events—their thickness, substance and, of course, *meaning*—only becomes clear in the mirror of memory, where they can be regarded in fuller context.

As if to bear witness to this, even our value judgments soften, become more understanding and nuanced, as events are regarded historically. Although I feel incapable of forgiving Alexander for the burning of Persepolis—just one of the many despicable acts in the history of the West, as I shall discuss later—I don't feel the blind fury and wailing despair I would have felt had I witnessed the barbarity unfold in real-time. With the distance and objectivity provided by the passage of time, I can put it in perspective, recognizing that Alexander was a product of his time and circumstances. He, too, was just human; and it is supremely difficult to be human. Judging him from the perspective provided by history allows me to discern the humanity I share with him more clearly, more in focus, and recognize that we are all potentially capable of heinous errors.

The past brings not only context, but also objectivity in how we regard life; an objectivity that is all but impossible in the rawness of the moment. As I write these words, the third year of Russia's war of choice on Ukraine rages on. There is no space in my heart—and frankly, there shouldn't be, neither in mine nor in any of my contemporaries' hearts—for understanding and compassion towards atrocious war criminals engaged in heinous barbarism. The present—when evil acts can still be stopped before fully developing—demands action and the emotional engagement that drives it, not contemplation and sober understanding; the latter is something only the distance and perspective provided by the past—when acts are *fait accompli*—creates space for and renders morally acceptable. This is *not* to say that (war) criminals should ever be divested of responsibility for their crimes; it only means that the sources and patterns of their actions (and possibly inactions) can be better discerned. For even the worst, most gratuitous acts of evil have hidden causes, twisted as those may be. Therefore, they should—*must*—be *comprehended* in retrospect; comprehended through an *objective* contemplation of the past, so we learn how to preempt the repetition of evil in the future. I shall speak more to this later in this book.

For now, though, what I mean by objectivity above is an ability to withdraw passional judgment. Just as we don't judge a pride of lions for bringing down an elephant and devouring it alive for hours on end, the passage of time, by taking the edge off our emotional responses, allows us to contemplate life with more sober discernment and compassion. Do we rage against ninth-century Vikings for their unmitigatedly brutal raids? Or thirteenth-century Mongols for their barbaric invasion of Europe? Hardly. Instead, we contemplate their human journeys from a less emotionally charged vantage point, and even find space in our hearts to be grateful for those among their deeds and cultural contributions that are deserving of appreciation.

The passage of time allows us to better discern the *totality* of life, synthesizing its many seemingly contradictory and dichotomous facets into a harmonious whole. The Western mind is uniquely capable of reading the past as if reading a heroic epic, a great novel, in which glory and despair, triumph and suffering, war and peace, are all integral to the drama, each contributing an indispensable note to the symphony of life.

The ability to discern glory in defeat, heroism in suffering, nobility in sacrifice, completeness in dichotomy, harmony in opposition, significance in banality, and meaning in absurdity, is the unique gift of time. To live only in the present moment is to reject this gift, something the Western mind intuitively understands. For we, Westerners, are constitutionally incapable of living only in the present. This is a blessing, not a curse; a birth right, not a liability; something to be embraced and celebrated, not rejected and overcome through decades of meditation. To eliminate time—the past and the future—from the crucible of the Western mind is a mutilation. What we need is to develop a mature, functional relationship with time—with the regrets and horrors of the past and the anxieties associated with the future—not cut it off from our lives. Whether we like it or not, *we have a past, and we have a future*; they are both integral parts of us right now.

The steady flow of lived moments into the past brings with it compassion for both victim and perpetrator, and can even—in a magical alchemical transmutation—turn suffering into loving kindness and sweet longing.

Here is a case in point. For reasons I'll share with you later in this book, my teenage years were excruciatingly difficult; a period of my life that my adult self has tried very hard to contain and forget. Visiting those rooms in the palace of my memories used to evoke deep anguish, and so I kept their doors well locked. Only in my late forties have I developed a more mature, kindhearted, compassionate relationship with my teenage self and his mighty struggle. And now, to my astonishment, I find myself even feeling a kind of sweet nostalgia for those times of suffering.

Allow me to unpack this a bit more, so you don't get the impression that I miss the brutality of suffering, because I don't. What I miss is the kid behind that suffering, the simplicity and spontaneity of his way of being in the world, his openness to life despite adversity, and his instinctive readiness to allow the world to imprint itself on him. For, as Rainer Maria Rilke wrote,

it is our task to impress this provisional, transient earth upon ourselves so deeply, so agonizingly, and so passionately that its essence rises up again 'invisibly' within us.

(*Letters on Life*, edited and translated by Ulrich Baer, The Modern Library, 2005, page 23)

I miss that kid's uncanny ability to find wonder in the smallest things. I miss *his* world—the world as he experienced it, even in the midst of his suffering—which isn't the world I experience today. Rilke again:

Deep on the inside everyone is like a church, and the walls are adorned with festive frescoes. In earliest childhood, when this magnificence is still exposed, it is too dark inside to see the images, and then, while the hall is gradually reached by light, adolescent foolishness and its false longings and thirsting shame set in and cover up the wall after all.

(*Ibid.*, pages 69–70)

Delightfully, however, since recently I have been able to re-evoke that past self—by listening to old songs and re-engaging with past interests—which somehow is still alive within me. I can again experience—briefly—the world through his eyes, reacquainting myself with the vibrancy and significance he saw in most things; things that my adult self has become numb to. I then experience great warmth and compassion for that kid. If I could speak to him across time, I'd tell him that his suffering, too, is an integral part of the beautiful painting of his life, something to be owned, cherished as a note in his unique song, not something to be hated and repressed. But he wouldn't understand it, for only time can allow for this understanding. Only time can help us see that suffering is part and parcel of the palette with which our lives are painted by nature; and that without it, we would end up a lesser work of art.

We cannot understand life in the present moment, but only in hindsight. Only time reveals the calm, warm splendor of personal suffering, for suffering is the engine of growth, insight, and even beauty. "Behind every exquisite thing that existed, there was something tragic. Worlds had to be in travail, that the meanest flower might blow..." wrote Oscar Wild (*The Picture of Dorian Gray*, Dover Publications, New York, 1993, page 26). Most importantly, *only time reveals the self*, for the self is a dynamic expression that doesn't exhaust itself in a mere moment. Instead, it needs time to unfold its inner complexity and nuances, so to reveal itself to itself.

To truly be *me*, I must thus remember and embody everyone I have been throughout my life, including the anguished teenager; the child who liked to climb mountains, tinker with computers, and who loved his father dearly; the young, wide-eyed materialist scientist who thought he could understand the universe; the energetic, ambitious and cold-hearted technology entrepreneur; the power-hungry corporate executive; the philosopher hoping to be wise one day; the author hoping to find his telos; the husband, the loving partner, the feline, the alien, the Other, the Daimon; *everyone*.

And even this is not enough: I must also remember and embody all those who were *before* me, and who now live in me, such as my father, my family, and—most importantly— my broader philosophical, spiritual family, which includes not only Jung, Schopenhauer, Spinoza, and Nietzsche, but also Søren Kierkegaard, Johann Wolfgang von Goethe, Immanuel Kant, Emanuel Swedenborg, Plato, Parmenides, and countless others. Their path is my path. To truly be *me*, I must embody and give expression to all who defined me and gave context to my existence; to all who now look over my shoulders in the hope that I will throw in my 2 cents and get all of us closer to our common telos. The true self is never a fluke of the moment, and neither is it ever alone. The true self is a dynamic, boiling collective. There is a crowd within each of us, looking out through our eyes and living life through our deeds.

There have been many individuals going by the name of Bernardo Kastrup. But most were lost by the wayside as the vehicle of my life moved inexorably forward. This happens to most of us: we lose pieces of ourselves along the way, without even noticing them. We are phenomenally cavalier about what we abandon, what we leave behind. A wheel cap falls unnoticed here, and exhaust pipe there, a whole door further ahead, until the vehicle of life starts to feel bare, empty, cold, and windy. Yet, to be our true selves we must remember, recover, and re-integrate all those fallen pieces of ourselves, as well as recognize the ancestors who live in them. The totality of being is a process that, despite existing in the present alone, reaches out across time and space so to stitch countless moments together in the cosmic synthesis of the here and now.

As such, it is true—as the Eastern mind has discovered before the Western mind was even born—that ultimately there is only the present. The problem is that the Western mind tends to misinterpret this assertion as meaning that the past and the future can be forgotten and ignored. Such misinterpretation is tragic: the present is the only thing that exists *because both the past and the future exist in the present, as integral parts of the present*. You have never experienced a past beyond your memories, which are themselves experienced now; always now.

You have never experienced a future beyond your expectations, which are themselves experienced now; always now. Therefore, to truly live the present moment in all its richness and breadth, in all its substance and depth, *we must integrate our memories and expectations, our history and aspirations.* In the language of the Western mind, we must embrace and embody the past and the future. To be our true selves, we must be the entire arrow of time. If you succeed in doing so, you won't feel empty or alone a day in your life. This is the great promise of the Western life.

But the challenge of living life *sub specie aeternitatis* — from the perspective of eternity, as Spinoza put it — is formidable. It forces us to confront both what we desperately reject about ourselves, and what we despise about the world. It demands that we integrate our traumas, regrets, shortcomings, fears, and the life unlived. That's why the archetype that reigns over Western life is, and has always been, that of the Hero. We must heroically reforge all this muck in an inner fire fueled by unconditional, inexhaustible vitality. Nietzsche — a man few could ever equal, let alone better — tried and succumbed, for ours is the daunting alchemical challenge of turning dung to gold.

If we must fail, then let us fail beautifully and meaningfully, as Nietzsche did. For failure, too, is archetypal and teleological; it has a unique quality and significance of its own, which is integral to the totality of being. Only by failing do we visit some dark cellars of the palace of mind, which would otherwise remain undiscovered and merely latent, like rocks unturned. Our failures are a service — a sacrifice — to nature, through which nature experiences the true force and poignancy of its own existence. Imagine a novel in which everything always goes well and all characters always succeed: how boring, unevocative and uncompelling; how flat and dull. No heroic epic can be devoid of failure, for failure is the extra dimension that gives depth to life. With attention, we can — and must — see the beauty that underlies failure.

The enormity of our challenge is the reason why we tend to flee from our own nature. We hear Eastern masters tell us that the antidote to suffering is to live only in the present moment and renounce the world. This is music to our escapist ears, for it gives us permission to repress and throw away all that we don't like about ourselves, our regretful past, our anxious future, and the sordid world that defines us. It gives us permission not to drink from the bitter chalice of a heroic life, a life of beautiful failures and overpowering suffering saturated with meaning, depth, and poignancy.

And so we convince ourselves that we aren't really Westerners, but instead Easterners in disguise. Their way is our way, a conclusion we can take seriously only because we fail to recognize the archetypal templates that define us. To cut a Western mind off from its past and future is a mutilation, a neutering of the eternal present, a form of spiritual bypassing. All we must recognize is that the past and the future are always *here*, right *now*, amenable to inquiry and integration, as opposed to being untouchable monsters playing with us as if we were remote-controlled marionettes. Younger than the Eastern mind as we are, and terribly confused as we have admittedly been, we still have our own path; one true to the Western mind.

In the Western path, we must confront head-on, and integrate in life, the greatest inevitability the future brings with it: our death. For our upcoming oblivion is also our spiritual ascension. By this I don't mean something metaphysical or abstract, but instead something very present and concrete: while alive, we are farting, sweating, stinky organisms; fragile, vulnerable, frightened little creatures perennially oppressed by the monstrosity of the world and fouled by myriad character flaws. But upon death, we take on the invulnerability and mythical glow of the ancestors. We become wholesome, no longer tainted by biological necessities or the banalities of eking out an existence. Our character flaws take a backseat—fade into the background—so the future can hear our contributions more clearly, with less noise and better focus.

When you think of the late Steve Jobs, do you think of an abusive, deeply unempathetic bully who eschewed his own daughter, or a visionary who put a dent in the universe and improved our lives? When you think of the late Arthur Schopenhauer, do you think of a supremely arrogant misogynist who despised his own mother, or a profound intellectual who pointed the way forward? When you think of the late Richard Wagner, do you think of a ghastly antisemite who lived with another man's wife, or the creator of otherworldly overtures that nurture our souls? When you think of the late Johann Wolfgang von Goethe, do you think of a clueless wannabe physicist who made a fool of himself pushing a ludicrous theory of light while wrongly—yet conceitedly—criticizing Sir Isaac Newton's, or the greatest poet, author, and polymath in the history of Germanic culture? Death erases mistakes, purifies, edifies, elevates our otherwise tainted legacies; it makes us more than merely human, clears the banal, the weak, the silly, the vulgar, the censurable, and brings forth the purity of what nature has achieved through us. Because of death, our legacy becomes more powerful than we could ever hope to be in life. For philosophers in particular, death frees the work from the life-stench of the worker, the ideas from their crude, precarious mouthpiece. Analogous reasoning applies to the rest of us as well: for instance, because of death, my own Danish ancestors weren't ragtag economic refugees, but—like Jason and the Argonauts—great adventurers who heroically crossed a vast ocean to fulfill their destinies. Death reveals life for what it truly is: an unfathomably compelling epic that no work of fiction could ever hope to match.

There is, thus, a strong sense in which we can only truly become ourselves—realize our full potential as individuals—

by dying. Just as death is oblivion when it lies in the future, it is also an apotheosis—a spiritual completion, the crowning of life—when it lies in the past. Here, again, time performs its alchemical miracle and blurs the distinctions between seeming opposites. Only our divorce from the past and the future—from the perspective of eternity—prevents us from seeing that, to fully *be* ourselves, *we must die*; just as much as we must be born. Until one dies, one hasn't fully *been.* For death is a coming into being at a higher, more vigorous level; it is the final, triumphant act of a teleological arch that imprints us into the crystal of eternity. To die in accordance with our destiny is the ultimate, indispensable goal of life, without which life would truly be just mundane.

The inheritance we've received from our ancestors means that we are never alone; nothing in our life—not even our procrastination, fears, regrets, and failures—is devoid of a point; the foundations of our being stretch so far below our feet that we cannot even hope to fathom them; and the death we so fear is the apotheosis of our being as much as our oblivion. Whether we understand or even believe this reality is as irrelevant as whether the apple blossom understands the tree from which it arises, and whose future it will unknowingly ensure. Finally, having an intimate relationship with this reality is our birthright as Western minds; it belongs in us.

Chapter 4

Pushed into Hades

When I was 12 years old, my father died of a sudden, fulminating heart attack. He was just 54. I remember that day with almost absolute clarity and vividness—I remember even individual words people said, and how they said them—for it was then that one Bernardo fell into the fires of Hades, so others could be forged anew.

Today, *sub specie aeternitatis*, I understand that my father's death was his greatest gift to me, his highest expression of love. For his parting act forced me into the world and granted me my great initiation into life—a rare thing in this age of comfort and accommodation, the age of the *Letzter Mensch* (last human) accurately predicted by Nietzsche. With his ultimate sacrifice, my father singlehandedly spared me such a miserable fate, described by Nietzsche thus:

the earth has now become small, and upon it hops the last human, who makes everything small.... One continues to work, for work is entertainment. But one takes care lest the entertainment become a strain. One no longer becomes poor or rich: both are too burdensome. Who wants to rule anymore? Who wants to obey? Both are too burdensome.... One has one's little pleasure for the day and one's little pleasure for the night ... "We have invented happiness"—say the last humans and they blink.

(*Thus Spoke Zarathustra*, translated by Graham Parkes, Oxford University Press, 2005, page 16)

By crowning his own through death, my father gave me *my* true life; his sacrifice forced me away from the warmth and comfort of the hearth and into the cold, monstruous world, so I, too, could fulfill my own fate. Without it, I would have lived a very comfortable, very predictable, and very mediocre life, the potentialities latent in me never fully flourishing.

But the medicine that secures the teleological arch of one's true life is often bitter beyond bearing. My father was the center of my existence; everything I did or felt orbited the power of his presence. He was already 42 years old when I was born, so I've never known a young, tentative, confused, or insecure father. Since as far back as I can remember, he radiated stability, self-confidence, and strength. And since he died too early for me to discern his weaknesses and character flaws, in my mind he will forever remain the *Übermensch*, never the *Letzter Mensch*. Losing him pulled the carpet from under my feet and threw me into a disorienting free fall of grasping despair.

Nobody else could ever play the role my father played in my life. He was the safe harbor I never dared to stray too far from. I knew that he knew how I felt and understood me. And he always had the exact right words to say in every moment of need, without patronizing or distancing himself from me. Nobody else could do it; certainly not my mother, who is vastly different from me in temperament. For her, too, my father was a father, not just a husband. And thus, his parting threw my mother into a spiral of despair of her own—one she never re-emerged from. Needing support herself, she could never help me cope with the brutality of my initiation. And that, too, from the perspective of eternity, was for the best: the welcoming lap of one's understanding mother can stop one from living out one's destiny.

I was my parents' only child together, thus my initiatory journey was entirely unaccompanied. And no other man in my life could radiate the presence my father did, in order to reassure me. In hindsight, I know I implicitly tried to, but never managed to project onto anyone else the energy of my father. Other men weren't truly adults the way my father was—I thought—but merely older "boys," confused and fallible like me. So losing my father was akin to losing *everyone*.

I also lost *everything* upon his passing, for I suddenly found myself in a surprisingly cold and alien world. Indeed, up to that moment my world had been colored by my father's presence. Without him, everything became instantly unrecognizable and distant. All that had hitherto been warm and familiar was unceremoniously taken away from me. Even if I had wanted to stay home—instead of setting out to the world, as I ultimately did—there was nowhere recognizable to stay; there was no home left. My initiation was complete, irrevocable, and absolute. All ties to the hearth were severed.

It's difficult to describe how I felt in the few years of darkness between my father's passing and the early dawn of my autonomy as a young adult. The word that comes to mind is "lack": the brutal absence of something essential to my very being. The obvious account of this feeling is that my teenage self was simply missing his beloved late father; and that, of course, was true enough. But even then, as a kid, I intuited that there was more to it. For recent as my father's passing was, this lack felt old, ancient even; it felt like a primordial memory, not a new experience. Whenever and wherever the beginning of all things was, this lack was already there—or so I intuited—as a perennial background to existence, merely obfuscated by the luminosity of my father's presence. I felt it physically as a hollow at the base of my throat and upper chest, a void that demanded to be filled and thus made me contract around it as if pulled inward. Without my father's presence, I had no defense against it, no shield, no escape; I had to endure it naked, every day, every hour, every minute. Every breath I took was a deliberate effort to inflate my ribcage against its inward pull.

As an adult, with my judgment no longer clouded by the emotional charge of loss, I could confirm the validity of my early intuitions: there is indeed a perennial, primordial lack underlying the Western mind; one that is simply obfuscated by our ephemeral flashes of victory, success, consumption, or whatever the distraction of the moment is. Throughout the ages, philosophers, scientists, and poets have spoken of different facets of this primordial lack, as well as the driving will to meet it, so completeness can finally be attained. For Charles Darwin, this was the frantic, competitive will to life; for Nietzsche, the irresistible will to power, embodied in the *Übermensch*; for Sigmund Freud, the embarrassing will to pleasure; for Jacques Lacan, the vague but felt will to *das Ding*, the unattainable thing; for Viktor Frankl, the foundational will to meaning that carries us through the very worst of life; and for John Donne, the ardent will to God. Only Jung seems to have formulated the more complete synthesis, in the form of the will to Self.

When things go south in our lives, we are prone to blaming mere circumstances or contingencies for the re-emergence of the ever-present primordial lack in the field of our attention. We are very good at conjuring up eminently reasonable causes for what is always with us, as part of us: we blame the economy, the boss, the partner, the weather, the neighbor, the death of the father. But it hardly ever occurs to us that the lack we feel *wasn't caused*; instead, it has always been present, sometimes more visibly, sometimes less so, but always there as an intrinsic part of us. We're simply put together this way, archetypally.

The Western life is surfed atop a forever-rolling wave of primordial lack. Paradoxically, this wave is what sustains and propels us forward, for in a state of total contentment we wouldn't care to lift an arm or achieve anything; life would lose its impetus, its drive, and grind to a frozen halt. Precisely *because* we lack, we act, we try, we fight, we risk, we thrash about, we advance, we screw up, we live... or we fall over the edge of the abyss. Either way, we don't stand still.

This is so Western—so intrinsic to us—that we don't see it; we take it entirely for granted, as a kind of self-evident universal. Worse yet, we think our felt lack is a problem to be solved. Only a non-Western mind can offer us the contrasts we need to discern our own outlines in the mirror. In his autobiography—*Memories, Dreams, Reflections*—Jung recalls what a Native American elder from the Taos Pueblo tribe, in New Mexico, once told him:

> How cruel the whites are: their lips are thin, their noses sharp, their faces furrowed and distorted by holes. Their eyes have a staring expression. They are always seeking something. What are they seeking? The whites always want something, they are always uneasy and restless. We do not know what they want, we do not understand them, we think that they are mad.
>
> (page 276 of the Fontana Press paperback edition, 1995)

There you go: that's us, our archetypal madness described back to us with illuminating clarity and disarming precision. We are restless, uneasy, always seeking something. And we seem to be structurally incapable of finding it, whatever it may be, for the seeking never ends. If that's how you feel, don't bother to look for causes, for *nothing* has caused it. You are simply a Western mind, made by nature just the way you are. And you can't escape it either: the primordial lack you feel is not a problem to be solved, but a template of being to be lived. We die seeking, in one of nature's most epic and magnificent failures.

What the Taos Pueblo elder didn't know—because it would have been inconceivable to him—is that *we, too, do not know what we seek.* All we know is that we must seek. And so we do, incessantly, tirelessly, because we cannot sit still in the felt presence of the primordial lack. It propels us forward by making life otherwise unbearable. Indeed, the primordial lack has propelled Alexander to conquer Persia, Galileo to invent empirical science, Europeans to colonize the Americas, Americans to land on the moon, engineers to create the Internet and AI, and so on. None of this has ever soothed a Western heart or quieted a Western mind, but we carry on anyway, acting out the only template we know to embody. It's our nature. And it's gloriously okay too.

We lack, and thus we push. But because we do not know what we lack, we push chaotically in all directions; we turn over every rock to see if what we find underneath can sooth our soul. We are energetic but clumsy, driven but unwise, and often ghastly destructive—just ask those we colonized or waged pointless wars against. Our felt lack propels us towards great good, but also great evil. Frankly, we are loose cannons on the ship of life on Earth. Our potential is great—we can be, and have been for a few centuries now, the global engine of human progress—but so is the danger we represent. Arguably, we're nature's greatest gamble on this planet. And we're young, with everything this entails. That's the part we got in the epic play of life on Earth.

Nature feels through us what it lacks. Existence is not a complete work of art; brushstrokes are still missing. Whatever the omitted elements are, they're ineffable, otherwise some philosopher or poet would have already written about them and thereby scratched the cosmic itch. Nonetheless, the missing brushstrokes can still be sensed, intuited, and nature senses them through us. There is some latent natural potential that has hitherto gone unexpressed, so nature tries—through us—to figure out what it is and express it; it tries to scratch its own cosmic itch through our hands, haphazardly as the case may be.

Because it is nature herself that feels and pushes through us, the energies we can mobilize in our chaotic search for wholeness are unfathomable. They have destroyed entire civilizations through Western colonialism and invented thermonuclear warfare. This is the danger implicit in nature's greatest gamble: applied without discerning moral oversight, its energies can be fantastically destructive. That's why the health of the Western mind's relationship with evil is so critical.

Unfortunately, we're still naïve when it comes to managing the evil latent in us. We think the way to go is to *avoid* engaging with it altogether; to reject any relationship with it, other than to push it away or destroy it. Astoundingly, we've even become *ashamed of understanding evil*, as if understanding could taint or foul us; as if understanding implied contamination, acquiescence, condonation, or exoneration. We think we might fall victim to evil if we were to study it intimately and actually grasp it. "Evil is over there, not here; here we cannot fathom what makes those devils do what they do," says the righteous family man. A few years later, he picks up an assault rifle and kills a dozen strangers in a shopping mall for no reason. By not understanding evil and its nuanced, seductive dynamic, our righteous family man made sure he had no defenses against it; not even an inner alarm to let him know that he was getting caught in the spell of evil. For most evildoers don't see themselves as doing evil. Hitler thought he was taking the Germanic peoples out of misery. Putin thought he was ensuring the safety and future prosperity of the Slavic peoples. Hernán Cortés, the most brutal Spanish conquistador, thought he was doing God's work. And so did the crusaders, the officials of the Inquisition, and the 9/11 terrorists. Evil isn't obvious to those caught in its spell. If we are to protect ourselves against it, we must understand how the spell works, how it insinuates itself, and how it eventually takes the reins of our lives. To be a Western mind *is* to carry this heavy moral responsibility, for the forces that nature mobilizes through and in us are immense. We are the titanic embodiments of Prometheus and have already stolen the power of fire from the gods.

Our juvenile pride in rejecting any attempt to understand evil is potentially catastrophic. For obviously *we cannot manage or control a process we do not understand*. This is so self-evident it hurts. *We must understand evil*, not only abstractly, but *intimately*. We must grasp what makes an evildoer tick, their outlook, motivations, the psychological rewards they reap from doing evil. We must be able to visit the rooms in the palace of mind that motivate evil acts, without losing ourselves in the process. And yes, I *do* see the obvious danger this entails—empathizing with evil may tickle dangerous, dormant potentials within us—but it is a risk we must take. For the alternative is to be at the mercy of evil while giving expression to the unfathomable, Promethean forces underlying the primordial lack that drives us.

In the few years following my father's passing, I tried my best to pin down what it was that I missed so intensely in the core of my being. Again, taking the obvious at face value—i.e., that I was simply missing my dead father—was something I both intuitively thought inadequate and didn't want to accept either; for accepting it would mean that my dilemma had no solution, as I couldn't bring my father back. You see, as a kid, I thought the primordial lack was a problem I could solve, and that solving it would make me feel whole and expansive again, like I once did. I thus had to figure out what I needed, so to work my way towards it. The alternative—I thought—was to roll up in a fetal position and wait to die in a corner.

Struggling with this question, I eventually felt compelled to return to the fabled European continent—"mother of all demons," as Jung once described it—so ubiquitous in family lore. I grew up thinking of Europe as a magical ancestral land—though rainy and prone to war—where my own roots had been laid even before I was conceived. If I were to go back to that point of origin, I thought, maybe I'd find the thread that could lead me back to what I had lost; maybe I'd even find a piece of my father along the way. The very idea of Europe became a beacon of hope for my young self. And although my surviving family couldn't help me cope psychologically with my father's absence, they had the resources and the willingness—particularly my maternal grandfather, a very old-fashioned, ultraconservative man with an understanding heart—to help with my journey. I think they were aware of their inability to comfort me in any other way, and so did the one thing they could do.

A part of me understood what was going on in my young mind: although I had failed to project my father's energy onto another person, I succeeded in projecting it onto the very land of Europe. As a matter of fact, by lineage I am overwhelmingly a combination of Iberian Celt and Northern Teutonic, a synthesis that made me associate Europe *as a whole* with identity and parenthood. I thus felt drawn to that point of origin as if it were a magical wellspring that, just as it had made me once, could reconstitute my wholeness. The logic here is precarious, I know, but the feeling was very real.

Nonetheless, I was by nature too self-critical to buy unreservedly into my own convenient narratives—especially after later realizing that being in Europe didn't, by itself, magically eliminate my sense of lack. I paid instinctive attention to the nuances of my feelings, and so eventually realized that there was more to soothing the primordial lack than some objective panacea out there in the world, regardless of continent. Two wonderful works of art helped me see this:

Tim Buckley and Larry Beckett's "Song to the Siren," sung in enchanting manner by Elizabeth Fraser (1983)—incidentally, I'm listening to it as I write these words and much of this book— and Krzysztof Kieślowski's cinematographic magnus opus *La Double Vie de Véronique* (1991). Inexplicably to me at the time, both drew tears out of me. As I wept, I couldn't for the life of me figure out *why* they made me long so intensely for something I couldn't even pin down; something simultaneously familiar and entirely unknown and inaccessible.

On one occasion, this feeling was not only disconcerting but embarrassing: I was with a girl in the cinema watching *La Double Vie*. There is a scene towards the end of the film when Véronique finds Veronika—the latter being a symbol of what Véronique needs to complete herself—in a photo she had taken years earlier, during a trip to Poland. Véronique then cries, for she realized how close, and yet how far away, she had unknowingly been to wholeness. Her crying prompted me to helplessly weep along with her, which was incredibly atypical for me. So when the girl who was with me completely failed to understand both the scene and my reaction to it, I felt deeply embarrassed. The confusion I saw stamped on her face made me want to bury my head in the ground like the proverbial ostrich. But the feeling never left me; not to this day, well over 30 years later.

I understood that scene; I knew what Kieślowski was hinting at. Véronique had just found the answer to her primordial lack, and it had her own face (both Véronique and Veronika were played by the same Swiss actress, the lovely Irene Jacob). What we so desperately lack—the thing that puts the entire ship of life in motion—isn't just some object or place out there; it has more to do with ourselves than we, at the present juncture in history, dare to imagine; it has our face and speaks with our voice. Yet, it isn't confined to the bag of skin we see in the mirror; instead, it's "smeared out" across the world. This ineffable something doesn't obey—doesn't care about—our conceptual categories, such as the distinctions we draw between subject and object, self and world. The focus of our passion—the *Logos*, the *Lapis Philosophorum*, the Beloved, the Father—is simultaneously self and other, inside and outside. We aren't quite ready yet, as a culture, to conceptualize this seeming paradox, but we surely can sense it through the intuitive roots that anchor us in reality. I surely did, and thus know that the answer to the primordial lack is as much in here as it is out there.

In the days and weeks immediately following my father's passing, family and friends were understandably concerned about my psychological wellbeing and sought to be close to me. They couldn't have known it but, with one single exception, their closeness felt oppressive to me. I secretly eschewed all attempts by others to father me; they felt preposterous, clownish, insulting like pathetic frauds, despite being well-meaning. What I needed was space, distance from the energy of mourning. My mother, despite—or perhaps *because* of—her own downward spiral of despair, also sought to be close to me. Today I understand her: I was the closest thing to my father that she had left in the world, and she desperately needed that solace. But a 12-year-old who had just lost his father was in no position to give anything to anyone, let alone solace. My mother's anxious, unstable, clingy energy was almost as difficult to bear as my own sorrow. Our differences in temperament became exacerbated and I just couldn't abide in her presence; it felt suffocating.

So I tried to distance myself from everything and everyone, if not physically—which wasn't under my control as a kid— at least psychologically. I needed to be alone in the crucible of my own mind, to deal with my own demons and, eventually, somehow find a way back to something resembling a life. As it happens, the only opportunity I consistently had to be alone with myself was in the darkness of the night, in bed, where I could pretend to be asleep so no one would come and try to "help." What I did every night then, for an hour or two before finally falling asleep, was something vaguely related to what we might call a "meditation." And it was during one of these spontaneous "meditations" that something as unexpected as it was befuddling happened to me for the first time.

I was once again trying to visualize a life without my father — to will it into existence in my imagination at least. As usual, I drew a blank and finally fell into quiet despair. My bed was positioned along a wall, so I spontaneously started punching the wall with the side of my right fist, not in frustration, but despondency. That was the deepest point in Hades I have ever visited; it was very, very dark, very hopeless, and thoroughly nihilistic. "It is all irremediably over, there's nothing left," was my thought.

And then, suddenly, a voice popped into my head, totally out of the blue. It was *my* voice, but not my usual tone. It said: "The boy *really* is desperate now..."

I was taken aback by this sudden and novel development. Don't get me wrong, the voice represented *my* subjectivity taking account of its own despair; it's just that, for some reason, it spoke of itself in the third person. *I* was the one thinking the underlying thought and saying the words in my own mind. I experienced the thought and the words from a first-person perspective; they didn't come from the outside. But the "me" doing it was an aspect of my mind that I didn't know — or even suspect — existed. It was completely calm and merely observing my own despair, from a standpoint outside the drama of my life. It wasn't a child, but ageless. It did experience the troubles of the kid but from "above," while the kid — the more familiar, egoic aspect of my mind — was being buried by his troubles. I hesitate to call it a dissociative state, as, again, I knew the whole thing was me, not an external agency. But this timeless aspect of my own mind was untouched by my troubles, seemingly invulnerable and, in this sense, indeed dissociated from my ego-self.

45

Over the following months and years, I learned to evoke that voice at will and even dialogue with it. I shall, from this point on, speak of it as an external agency because it was indeed external to my ego, and it's just easier to speak of it that way. But please remember that it wasn't an agency outside my own subjectivity; it was simply a hitherto undiscovered aspect of myself. I shall call it "the Other."

The Other knew better than to reassure me in the silly and patronizing ways adults tried to. He didn't use cheap, overtly shallow clichés like "everything is going to be alright" and the like. He knew I was in for some very, very difficult years, and didn't try to dismiss or minimize the suffering associated with it. What he did was to quietly reassure me that there was something on the other side of this long, dark tunnel I had just entered: a fate to be fulfilled, a purpose to be achieved, a path to be lived. Yet, he also knew that the suffering ahead was inevitable; I just had to go through the motions, there was no way around it. So the best thing to do was to put my head down and work hard, taking one step at a time, with endless patience and discipline. What I needed wasn't a solution, but simply to move forward, driven by a form of faith in the Other.

This hard work consisted of going through the usual steps required for becoming an autonomous adult: studying and graduating from school, getting into a good University, then studying some more and earning a degree, finding a good job, making money, building a reputation, etc. I decided then and there that I should regard these steps as a kind of suspension of life: I didn't need to enjoy them or even regard them as dignified; I just needed to go through them, tick the boxes, so to get to the other side of the tunnel and finally live my true calling. Enjoyment and meaning were unimportant in this early phase. All that was required was to carve out a space in the world for myself; a platform from which I would eventually be able to project my influence onto the world; a base or foundation that would give me the independence, time, energy, and resources to finally be able to pursue my true destiny, whatever that might be. There was no shortcut to it. This is what the Other told me, and I heeded his advice without reservation.

You probably can imagine how serious a kid I then became. Except for the odd girlfriend or two, nothing I did during those years was for personal gratification; indeed, I hated much of it. But the inner voice of the Other reassured me that traversing that gauntlet was my inevitable fate, fighting it was pointless, and that one day I would understand why. That gave meaning to my misery and impetus for me to rise out of bed in the morning. Looking back, I realize I was never truly a teenager; that part of life wasn't in the cards for me. While other kids slowly became acquainted with the delights of the grown-up world, I just did what I had to. And in the empty moments of rest, when there was nothing left to do but wait alone for the motions of the world to catch up with me, I contemplated the infinite emptiness within, the ancestral lack in my chest and throat, dragging me into myself, making me small. I grew so familiar with that inward pull that I can easily evoke it at will, even right now, as I write these words. It's been a long-time companion of mine, family even. It's always there in the background, reliably, unfailingly.

Despite my early realization that Europe, in and of itself, couldn't magically make me feel whole again, my desire to surrender myself into the arms of the mother of all demons was compounded by another early realization: like my father, I am by nature an unambiguous individualist. I *must* live in my own unique way and terms, and just can't do otherwise. I find it impossible to sacrifice my own inner voice and compass so to conform to external expectations or fit into a mold. I never felt any desire to tell others how they should live, but I also never allowed anyone to dictate to me how I should. And my father was just like me: he, too, lived in his own unique way, and pursued his own unique interests.

Indeed, my father's various interests enriched my childhood enormously. He was an architect by education and worked for the city administration of Rio de Janeiro as an urban planner. But that—since as far back as I can remember—took only two days of his time per week. The rest of the time he would divide between his own private architecture practice and his many hobbies. He liked to build and fly remote-controlled model aircraft, kept tropical fish, maintained a sprawling HAM radio station, built electronic projects, and studied philosophy. These two latter interests would be pursued by me at a whole other level in my adulthood, but the seed of my interest in both traces back to my father. It was by being by his side as he built sound-effect machines, little radio transmitters, remote-control circuits, power supplies for my video games consoles, etc., that I developed my taste for the smell of molten solder (unless you are an electronics hobbyist from childhood, you cannot hope to understand why such a toxic smell is so magical). Also, it was his interest in philosophy that validated my own, for I had always secretly entertained deep philosophical questions in my mind that I didn't dare to discuss with my peers.

My father gave full expression to his own individual interests and pursuits, never sacrificing them in the name of external expectations. Looking back, I realize that he hardly had friends, only hobby mates. With one exception—a younger man who shared with my father an interest in philosophy, and who was the only person I felt comfortable talking to immediately after my father's passing—he didn't have a gang of pals to regularly talk to or go out with. The people he met with at the airfield to fly model airplanes only met him in those circumstances; the people who shared with him an interest in electronics only met him in that particular context; and so on. His individuality had center stage, everything else orbiting around it, in specific compartments.

This may sound entirely ordinary to you, and it indeed *is*, for you're likely as much a Western mind as my father was. But although Rio de Janeiro is largely a Western city, because it was shaped by immigration—or so I speculate—it developed a strong social peculiarity: a tribe-based social culture. By "tribe" here I don't mean anything primitive or derogative; I use the word simply because it is the most descriptively precise for what I mean. You see, for myriad immigrants arriving from all over the world, Rio didn't feel like home at first. Upon disembarking in Rio's old port, new arrivals would have been confronted with people who looked different and spoke a strange language. A natural self-defense mechanism under such circumstances is to close ranks around your own tribe: your friends and family, people you know personally. And so a culture emerged in Rio in which loyalty to your tribe—not society at large—was the only security guarantee one had. People would sacrifice their own individuality in order to fit into their respective tribes, for in a moment of need only one's tribe would come to the rescue. Indeed, unlike in Europe, the people of Rio weren't unified by a centuries-old national identity, language, and history, so they had to forge alternatives.

I discovered this only after my father's passing, for when one is very young one experiences one's own family much more than the culture at large. Because I grew up to be an individualist just like my father, I paid a price during my early teen years for my unwillingness to sacrifice my natural dispositions in the name of tribal loyalty. For instance, friends from school would sometimes show up at my door and tell me that "we're all going to the beach right now, let's go!" fully expecting me to join. But sometimes I was busy with something else or just didn't want to go to the beach—my skin burns much faster than it tans, so spending an afternoon at the beach was synonymous with pain—and would thus politely decline the invitation. To my astonishment, my friends consistently interpreted that to mean that I wasn't really one of the gang and couldn't be relied upon. This made me grow weary of inserting myself into any social group, as I knew they would demand from me a sacrifice of individuality that I was constitutionally incapable of making. So I drifted across tribes, friendly with all of them but never really becoming part of any; and they all knew it. In Rio, this meant that, in times of trouble, I had only myself to count on.

At first, I thought something was wrong with me. I thought my inability to be part of a "gang" was a weakness, reflected a lack of social skills, or even a form of morally reprehensible egocentrism. The culture around me certainly encouraged such an interpretation. But in fact, there was nothing wrong with me at all; I was just born an uncompromisingly Western mind, instinctively committed to the peculiarities of my own uniqueness. For no two human beings are ever the same. Nature tries something different through each one of us, expressing different admixtures of its inherent potentialities. Europe, in my mind, offered the hope of a society where I wouldn't be punished for owning my individuality.

Indeed, in a Western society, one must first be *oneself* before being able to contribute to the collective; otherwise, what would one have to give? Westerners aren't numbers or mere drones condemned to conformity in some Orwellian dystopia. We aren't just standard, replaceable cogs in a communist or fascist machine meant to express the individuality only of its leader, to the detriment of everybody else's. Instead, we are all *unique individuals* in our own right, and only through our individuality can we allow nature to do through us what it seeks to do. Only through the expression of what is inimitably ours do we have something of value to contribute. Such is the Western path.

Rio offered the social contrasts that helped me discern this Westerness in me, and then in others. As such, being born there gave me an outside perspective into myself, allowing me to recognize what many Westerners take for granted, aren't explicitly aware of, and therefore hardly value. My early years in that faraway, exotic land — which sometimes feel like a dream to me today — gave me a unique standpoint from which to contemplate the power and purpose of my individuality.

Individual expression is the engine of the West. We feel the unique push of nature rising from deep within us; a push that others have variously called fate, destiny, calling, vocation, lot, etc. Whatever we call it, it is as individual as a fingerprint or a face, and for the same reasons too. It can overcome all external pressures towards normality and conformity. Even if we rationally believe that the best life-path is the one culture and social expectations lay before us, something in us rebels, screams, trashes about until we hear it and adjust our course accordingly. As psychologist James Hillman put it, there is a unique oak tree trying to grow from the acorn we start as. Its push is almost irresistible; and when it *is* resisted, one pays a steep price in the form of regret, ennui, anxiety, and even physical illness.

It was Steve Jobs's uncompromising individuality that largely defined how we produce and consume information in the early twenty-first century. He looked around and saw a world that didn't fit his idiosyncratic taste, so something had to give. As a true Western individual, he then figured that it wasn't Steve Jobs that needed to conform to the world, but the world that had to receive Steve Jobs's vision. And the vision trying to express itself through him was as divorced from social expectations as it was overwhelming. Without a formidable degree of maturity that very few humans can muster, the unavoidable side-effect of this dynamic was Jobs's well-known character flaws: he wasn't the unempathetic bully he was because he chose to or was proud of; *he just couldn't help it.* The urgency of his individual vision to express itself was more powerful than social norms or molds. Steve Jobs didn't have a unique vision; *his unique vision had him*. He was tossed around by the force of what nature was trying to accomplish through him in a manner that very few can plausibly hope to control. It wasn't his fault, for our natural individuality has us; we are tools of its expression, not the other way around. Sometimes, not even the love of our children can overcome this reality, as Jobs found out early in his life. Such is the power of nature's will to individual, unique expression in a Western mind.

Short of being killed—as Giordano Bruno was, burned alive at the stake by the Church for refusing to conform to dogma or recant his individual views about cosmology—few Western minds paid a higher price for their individualism than Spinoza. Born in Amsterdam in the Portuguese Jewish community, his tribe was his world. Portuguese was his mother tongue and the language he used in daily life. His Dutch is said to have been functional, but deficient enough that he felt embarrassed by it. All his prospects for earning a living were also tied to his tribe. Yet, he valued his own individual thought so much that he refused to conform to the norms and dogmas of his tribe. At one point, he was even offered a yearly stipend that would have guaranteed his subsistence, if only he would conform—at least outwardly—to his tribe's costumes and religious outlook. He refused and was then excommunicated and cursed by the Portuguese Jewish authorities. He was banned and forbidden to ever interact with members of his former tribe, even his own family. Spinoza thus gave up *everything* to remain true to his individual vision; so much so that, in his latest biography, Ian Buruma speaks of his "total commitment to individual autonomy and freedom" (*Spinoza: Freedom's Messiah*, 2024).

In more recent memory, Jung was perhaps the supreme example of Western individualism. He never compromised on it, remaining resolutely faithful to the unique vision that had him, even before he understood what was going on. For instance, towards the end of his university course in medicine, he had to choose a specialty. Because of his family's precarious financial situation, he knew that his choice had to be governed by short-term career and financial prospects. As such, internal medicine was the way to go, as market demand for it is unconditional and clinics were numerous. All of Jung's peers and teachers fully expected him to choose internal medicine; indeed, they had no doubt that he would. Yet, because of two peculiar dreams he had, Jung ended up choosing to become a psychiatrist—*Irrenarzt* in German, which means "doctor of the crazy"—a specialty frowned upon by his peers and teachers, and which offered very limited professional opportunities. That was his unique vocation and fate, contrary to all social expectations. Jung didn't actually choose psychiatry; psychiatry chose him. Psychiatry is what nature wanted to do through Jung and resisting the power of nature is a tall task. We, Westerners, are often helpless in the face of nature's unique vision for us. Yet, this is precisely what makes us valuable, unique individuals.

Later in life, already established as a great psychiatrist and scholar, Jung continued to express his individuality uncompromisingly. His writings antagonized the Church and were even considered heretical. He also maintained an open relationship with two women at the same time: his wife and a professional colleague. That this scandalized Swiss society wasn't enough to drive Jung to even be discreet about it, let alone surrender to conformity. Carl Gustav Jung, just like each one of us, was a unique individual, a unique expression of nature. And Western minds instinctively value such uniqueness as the very currency of nature's wealth.

My own life has been no different. I have been so many things over the years, apparently without rhyme or rhythm, in a path contrary to any reasonable social mold: computer engineer, nuclear scientist, entrepreneur, academic, corporate executive, philosopher, author, vintage computer conservator, publisher, electronics educator, editor, etc. Except for the very first step—i.e., becoming a computer engineer—social norms and expectations encouraged none of this. The uniqueness of my individuality was my guide at every twist and turn, for little of what I did conformed to the predictable, linear paths society had anticipated for me. Indeed, we are subliminally told that a regular life is the way to go, the mold to conform to: one graduates, gets a job in one's field, climbs the corporate ladder, raises children, retires, and goes off to play golf. The zigzagging, changes, and sharp turns that characterized my life were guided by my individual inner compass alone. I followed *my* path, not that of compliance. And I did so not because I chose to, but because my path chose me. This is how the Western mind operates, even when it is forced to compromise somewhat to secure its own subsistence.

As I write this, at the closure of the twenty-first-century's first quarter, the world provides formidable contrasts to Western individualism: Russian men, young and old, are cavalierly plucked from their families and careers, with utter disregard for their individual dispositions, vision, and circumstances, to be thrown as uniformed cannon fodder toward Ukrainian artillery. They are treated as mere numbers, throwaway tools, standard drones to be disposed of in the interest of some egomaniacal geopolitical abstraction in Vladimir Putin's sick mind, not as unique individuals. If they die, it's no problem—or so the thought goes—for people devoid of uniqueness can always be replaced, just as the cogs in a machine can be replaced with identical ones when they wear off. The Russian government's disregard for the value of *individual human lives*—even when they are those of their own men—contrasts unambiguously with the Western mindset in this regard. And things weren't very different in earlier Soviet times either: the Soviet government's disdain for individuality could be seen even in their architecture, with most people living in vast, uniform housing blocks, entirely devoid of character or uniqueness. That everybody lived in mass-produced standard housing was a symbol of the notion that people are all effectively the same, not only in regard to rights and opportunities, but also in their very essence and fate. Soviet communism saw individual human lives as replaceable pawns, the antithesis of individualism. Xi's China, in turn, tolerates individualism only insofar as it doesn't threaten or interfere with Xi's own authoritarian vision, under which his people, too, are standardized tools of the state, replaceable cogs in a machine. A look into how Chinese mega-factories operate can illustrate this very powerfully. Even in the geographical west, authoritarian populist forces—fundamentally anti-Western in nature—are in movement. They misuse freedom to achieve the end of freedom.

Freedom: that's the keyword. For individuality can only flourish when it has the freedom to unfold. Individual freedom is the quintessential Western value: the freedom to live and express ourselves as nature wants to live and express itself through us, uniquely, provided only that we do not interfere with the freedom of others to do the same. Nature must be free to do what it must—with moral oversight, of course—and it must do a great many unique things; it must turn over the rock of every one of its intrinsic potentialities. That's why Western countries attract so many outsiders: the latter—Western minds themselves—yearn for the freedom to be themselves and express themselves in their natural, unique ways. The West provides fertile ground where individual human expression can flourish. To a large extent, this is the basis of our economic prosperity: we allow people to tap into an endless wellspring of vitality and creativity when their individual nature isn't repressed but, instead, nurtured and empowered. All the great companies of the early twenty-first-century—Apple, Microsoft, Alphabet, NVIDIA, Amazon, Meta, Qualcomm, ASML, SpaceX, etc.—sprung from the movements of individual creativity—

entrepreneurship—nurtured by individual freedom. And so did all of our art and philosophy.

Western individualism is often misinterpreted and misrepresented—particularly by non-Western state actors—as synonymous with self-absorption and lack of compassion. But nothing could be farther from the truth. Let us take my own adopted country, the Netherlands, and the Scandinavian countries as examples: although they are all quintessentially Western, they also have the strongest social safety nets in the world. Citizens of these countries do not need to worry about being able to afford healthcare, feed their families if they lose their job, or care for themselves when they get old. Their fellow citizens make sure—through tax contributions and the government apparatus—that they are supported in case of need, irrespective of their personal acquaintances. In other words, when push comes to shove, *the entire country is their tribe*. I don't need to be personally acquainted with my neighbors down the street to contribute to ensuring their wellbeing when disaster strikes. Indeed, strong social safety nets are possible precisely because, in the absence of tribal loyalty directed only at the microcosm of personal acquaintances, citizens contribute to society as a whole, sharing the social burdens at a much larger and sustainable scale.

Sure enough, there are Western countries where such safety nets are weak, such as the USA. But my point is that individualism does not, by itself, contradict compassion; and neither is it synonymous with self-absorption. On the contrary: individualism allows compassion and social engagement to expand well beyond the confining boundaries of tribes. Moreover, often what makes strong social safety nets—the ultimate in compassion and engagement—possible is the economic prosperity generated precisely by the creativity and power unlocked by individual expression, in the form of entrepreneurship.

Western minds are driven by nature's immanent primordial lack, which they sense and are affected by to a greater degree than most. They frantically seek to express meaning in a manner that embeds them in the world, motivated by the instinctive hope of finding wholeness beyond the boundaries of the self. The way they go about this epic search is different and unique to each one of them—it is fundamentally *individual*—which reflects nature's multi-pronged attempt to scratch the cosmic itch. Indeed, the teleological arch that orients Westerners is as idiosyncratic as their fingerprints. Ultimately, however, whether personal wholeness is achieved or not isn't the most important question; what truly matters is what comes into being—what is *expressed* or *brought into reality* out of mere potentiality—during the search.

Chapter 5

The Anabasis of Orpheus

It was a midsummer Monday, just outside Geneva, Switzerland, when I woke up well before my alarm went off because a very special day lay ahead. Peeking through the curtains of my little third-floor studio, I could still see the brightest stars up in the sky, the silhouette of the Jura mountains vaguely discernible against it. The smell of the previous night's celebratory dinner — fried chicken cooked in riot fashion by some Italian friends — was still in the air, betraying how little sleep I had gotten. But I could hardly contain my excitement, as that was going to be my first day officially working at CERN — the European Organization for Nuclear Research — an almost mythical place where humans push the bleeding edge of knowledge. Indeed, CERN was — and still is — the world's cathedral of experimental high-energy physics.

As a kid, I had learned about the existence of that place from browsing the science magazines my father subscribed to. The notion that scientists could break up particles by smashing them together so to uncover the secrets hidden within — as if cracking a clam to find pearls inside — was every bit as inspiring to my child-mind as space travel. For I sensed — in an archetypally Western, alchemical intuition — that the mysteries of nature were as immanent in the matter at hand as transcendent in the above-and-beyond. As such, matter itself was saturated — I intuited — with mystery to be unveiled and meaning to be discerned, if only we knew how to crack its hard shell open. I thus formed the intention, quite early in life, to one day join the magical scientific pursuit at CERN so to help find the hidden pearls. And then suddenly there I was, about to realize my childhood dream already in my *very first job*. I wasn't quite yet 22 years old, drunk with anticipation, and expansive like a star about to go supernova.

That moment marked my re-emergence from Hades and return to the world of the living. Like the mythical Orpheus, I had failed to bring Eurydice—the Beloved, Veronika, she who restores one's wholeness and soothes the primordial lack— with me from the depths of hell, but this fact was entirely obfuscated by the brightness of the sun of life. And it would remain obfuscated still for years to come, for what mattered at that point was that *I was alive again, at long last!* I could see the world in colors once more and bask in the clarity and warmth of the noon's sun.

I even found a father figure in my boss, physicist Rudolf "Rudy" Bock, leader of the RD11 collaboration under the auspices of which I had completed my dissertation prior to officially joining CERN. I don't think I projected my late father onto him—as I mentioned earlier, I was never able to do that—but saw in him a separate father figure and mentor in his own right. My respect for that man, and acceptance of his mentorship, were spontaneous like fate. I looked up to him a lot and even got secretly upset when others—amongst whom his own "boss," the feared Marzio Nessi—spoke to him in a less-than-deferential tone ("How dare they?" I'd silently mutter). Looking back as I write these words, I realize that I loved that man. Cruelly, however, Rudy, too, would pass away unexpectedly several years later, forever ending my relationship with external embodiments of the Father and Old Wise Man archetypes. He was larger than life, and I miss him greatly.

CERN and the dramatic landscapes of Switzerland drew out of me my previously bottled-up but now free, gushing love for the world. Everything was beautiful again, embodied, concrete, luminous, pregnant with mystery and significance. I wanted to climb and touch every mountain, swim in every river, savor every wine, feel the skin of every attractive girl. At work, I sought to participate in every experiment, take part in every discussion, and help with every research effort. I once overheard Rudy describe me as *außerordentlich eifrig* ("exceptionally eager"), which I wasn't sure was meant as praise or criticism, but which was clearly a correct assessment either way.

As an experiment-oriented organization, everything done at CERN was embodied—as opposed to the abstractions of theory—and aimed at uncovering the secrets of the matter that palpably surrounds us. This attracted me, pulled me out of the world of the dead, and engaged me with life again. I loved touching the equipment, turning the knobs, connecting the cables, collecting printouts, pouring over the data, attending to every trace in every monitor and gauge. All of it was concrete, material, present, and yet deeply mysterious. For what we were doing—namely, looking for the Higgs Boson—aimed at accounting for a fundamental mystery of matter: the origin of inertial mass, the defining characteristic of everything we colloquially refer to as "material." Never had I felt so engaged with the concreteness of the world at so many levels. In a sense, I was making love with matter in all its nuances and layers of meaning, overt and otherwise. It was a unique time, which personal tragedy had primed me for.

There is an anecdote I want to share here, for it illustrates well my inner attitude at the time. At CERN, every scientist is expected to do a so-called "shift" every now and then. These shifts consisted of sitting for 4 hours in the control room of one of the several active experiments, monitoring all the variables of relevance, filing the collected data, and taking corrective action in case something deviated from the norm. This was merely technical work that anyone with half a brain could do, so most of us regarded it as an annoyance. The most dreaded shift, for obvious reasons, was that between midnight and 4:00

a.m. (once on, particle accelerators cannot be casually turned off, so they have to operate day and night for the duration of the experiment). Everybody and their grandmother would go to great lengths to swap that shift with someone retarded enough to volunteer. Guess who was always willing to do so? Yes, and I collected some handsome favors for it, even though the shift itself already delighted me enough: to have my hands on the controls, watch in real-time as particles deposited their energy on measurement surfaces according to spectacular—yet predictable—patterns, and basically *feel* the experiment as it unfolded. I just loved it, for it grounded me, made my work feel real.

Reflecting on all that, I rhetorically wonder: is there anything more Western than love for the concreteness of the physical world and engagement with its matter? "Engagement" is the salient word here. Westerners, by nature, seek to *engage* the world of things, the concrete world of matter. Only later in life, jaded by disappointments and exhausted of suffering, do we sometimes try to disengage, abandon the world by following Eastern masters and meditating our way away from everything. But this is an adaptive mechanism, a coping strategy, not a spontaneous, natural disposition. By trying to disengage from the world what we are *actually* trying to accomplish is to disengage *from suffering*; we just want to stop the shitshow, which couldn't be more human and understandable; it doesn't mean that we no longer feel drawn to the world. But since we wrongly associate most of our suffering with the circumstances and contingencies of the world, we get confused about our true goals.

Let us be honest: the Western love affair with matter is one of our most defining characteristics. I don't mean by this that Westerners are intrinsically predisposed to *metaphysical* materialism; for under such a grotesque fantasy matter is supposed to be pure abstraction, devoid of any intrinsic quality, which is precisely the opposite of how we are predisposed to regarding it. Our religious history also shows that metaphysical materialism has never been truly dominant in the Western mind. But regardless of metaphysics—regardless of our intellectual, conceptual positions concerning the nature or essence of matter—we are surely predisposed to engaging with this space we colloquially refer to as "the material world." We love beautiful *things*, objects, embodied concreteness. The economic success of capitalism in the West rests precisely upon this predisposition of ours. We live our lives in the context of matter and largely couch their meaning in it: the home that cradles us, the car that empowers us, the art that moves us, the places that inspire us, the clothes that represent us, the things we create and thereby embody us, and so on.

Somehow, the Western mind can see magic in mere things, thereby falling in love with them. We continue to intuit what, according to Owen Barfield, early humans quite spontaneously did too: namely, that

> there stands behind the phenomena, and on the other side of them from me, a represented which is of the same nature as me. Whether it is called 'mana,' or by the names of gods and demons, or God the Father, or the spirit world, it is of the same nature as the perceiving self, inasmuch as it is not mechanical or accidental, but psychic and voluntary.
>
> (*Saving the Appearances: A Study in Idolatry*, Barfield Press, 2011, page 42)

In other words: we see magic in things—the "phenomena" of the world, in Barfield's language—because we intuit that they represent a reality of the same nature as ourselves. Just as "behind" our material body there stand the thoughts and feelings of a person, so "behind" material things—which are made of the same types of elementary particles and fields that make up our body—there stands the inner life of a non-personal, non-individuated field of subjectivity. Underneath appearances, the world is our kin: it represents an underlying reality as alive as us, with its own intrinsic qualities and meaning. Although metaphysical materialism has largely driven this notion out of our intellect, it remains alive and vibrant in the deeper, intuitive, feeling-toned layers of our Western mind, covertly but powerfully modulating how we relate to the material world.

I am no exception to this. Even though my material ambitions today are relatively modest and largely unrelated to social status, I, too, find magic in the computers I design, build, and restore in my home. There is a sense in which they are enchanted objects, embodiments of an immanent order whose organizing impulses are channeled into the world through my hands. There is a certain numinosity in the matter that gives them form. For this reason, I delight in touching them, working on them with my hands in palpable, felt engagement. Moreover, I sense an immanent order in other material forms too, such as landscapes, mountains, fast-flowing rivers, and even mere pebbles, all shaped by the spell of nature's Overmind. Matter is pregnant with mystery and meaning; it's no coincidence that the word derives from *mater*, the Proto-Indo-European for "mother."

In our individuality, each of us has a different, unique relationship with matter. My partner, for instance, is a visual artist: the *forms* in her paintings are the expressed, embodied meaning of her life. She is also an organic gardener, regularly sinking her hands into the dark, moist, fertile soil of the lowlands to bring to *life* the foods that give us nourishment. Steve Jobs, in turn, related to matter in a largely *functional* manner, seeking not only the right form, but also the right behavior. He channeled this archetypal Western drive so well that the phones, tablets, and computers he produced have become objects of sensuous fetish. More generally, anyone who enjoys an artisanal craft is in a magical, yet concretely felt, creative relationship with matter. And so is any maker, builder, restorer, or collector, regardless of what they make, build, restore, or collect. What unifies us all is not the particulars of our relationship with matter, but *that* we all have a magical relationship with it.

There is an immanent significance to matter that the Western mind senses, recognizes, and proceeds to fall madly in love with. Absent metaphysical judgment—i.e., absent the current mainstream physicalist view that matter is pure abstraction, has no essence, depth, meaning, or intrinsic qualities—there is nothing wrong or unnatural about it; it's just the way nature made us, as well as matter itself. Granted, the Western orientation to matter can become dysfunctional if it turns into an addiction or obsession. But this risk is always there, whatever our natural orientations are. For example, religion, too, can become dysfunctional in the form of fundamentalism. So, if we are to be ashamed of something, it should be of our exaggerations and obsessions—the way we *handle* our dispositions—not our natural dispositions themselves. From the point of view of the Western mind, matter naturally matters; and it does so beautifully, seductively, irresistibly. There is something about matter that seems to suggest a tantalizing solution to the primordial lack. It sings the siren song of wholeness, and we can hear it.

Indeed, if my magical time at CERN has taught me any one great lesson, it is this: *there is absolutely nothing banal or prosaic about matter;* the mystery of what happens within a single proton is boundless. A single atom is an inscrutable universe of unknowns, despite all of our progress. High-energy physics has only scratched the surface of this mystery, and everything we have learned thus far has been an endless series of counterintuitive surprises. Strictly speaking, we don't quite know what matter is. All we know is that, whatever it turns out to be, it isn't trivial or trite. The alchemists knew this intuitively, and that's why they dedicated their lives to the exploration of the mysteries of matter. Subatomic physics is the cave of the Cumaean Sibyl: a realm where great secrets lie hidden, undisturbed by the power of today's particle smashers. Perhaps the uncanny beauty of super-symmetry—which we affectionately called "SuSy" at CERN—lurks there in wait, hiding at energy levels we are presently unable to reach. Or perhaps something else, inconceivable to the theoretical imagination of humans, sleeps silently in the microscopic labyrinths of the cave.

Whatever the case may be, the Western love affair with matter is not dismissible, frivolous, or mere projection of the ignorant. On the contrary: science shows us that the depth and mystery we sense in the heart of matter are real. The alchemical gold, brought about by the *Lapis Philosophorum*, represents an authentic enigma; one that is yet to be deciphered or corralled into the confines of human reason. Until it is, who is to tell us that our attraction to the enchantment of objects is misguided? Who is to tell us that the only important mysteries are otherworldly, when we don't know even what a mere grain of salt truly is? Why should imagined mysteries be more real or relevant than concrete and touchable ones, which we can hold in our hands? William Blake understood this, in true Western fashion:

> To see a World in a Grain of Sand
> And a Heaven in a Wild Flower,
> Hold Infinity in the palm of your hand
> And Eternity in an hour.
> ("Auguries of Innocence," 1803)

It is *how* we go about our relationship with matter that defines the quality of our Western lives, not *that* we have such a relationship. For instance, a throw-away culture is not one that respects matter; on the contrary. To treat objects as discardable commodities, accumulating in ever-growing landfills, doesn't do justice to the depths of meaning we intuitively sense in them. And neither does hoarding. To intuit the mystery immanent in matter is to have a sensuous, reverent, even ritualistic relationship with objects as *symbols of meaning*—i.e., as the visible representations of something that lie beneath superficial appearances. When a carpenter reverently runs his fingers over a wooden surface, feeling its texture and grain, he is having just such a sensuous, ritualistic relationship with the object of his art, which embodies and represents the meaning of his life. That Jesus was a carpenter tells us something about the deeper dispositions of the Western mind in this regard.

To honor matter is to treat it as an outer representation of something inwardly meaningful. Only then can matter be allowed to be to us what it is to itself: the discernible facet of divinity, the perceptible body of God. To relate to matter as an artist relates to their work, an artisan to their craft, a conservator to their charge, a Japanese *teishu* to her tea, or a priest to his iconography, *is to live surrounded by a world of significance*; a world with an extra dimension: depth of meaning. This world comes alive by the grace of what we sense in it, and then amplify through our reverent and receptive inner attitude towards it.

Think of it as the inner attitude we adopt—or rather, slide spontaneously into—in the presence of very material religious symbols, such as the statues and paintings in a church or temple, and even the building itself: something subtle changes within us, even if we rationally reject the significance of the symbols. Our inner chatter gives way to a degree of silence and solemnity, a spontaneous readiness to abide in a field of meaning. We become more alert, although without any particular focus of attention. Our consciousness shifts to a more receptive state, as if we were trying to hear the silent whispers of the symbols, the message of the represented behind the material representations.

The thing is, *all matter*—not just religious symbols—*can have this same effect on us*, if only we adopt a receptive attitude to it. The whole physical world can become an endless field of meaning, whispering its secrets to those who pay attention. *This* is the potential power of matter in the Western mind. Unlike some (Middle-)Eastern traditions, in which iconography is often discouraged or forbidden for the sake of unmediated access to transcendence, we are inherently predisposed to sensing the represented *through* the representation, thereby intuiting the extra dimension of meaning that provides depth to all material objects.

I've become explicitly aware of this thanks to two personal traits discovered late in my life: my attraction to churches—which, for the longest time, I attributed to an innocuous interest in their architecture, but which I now know to reflect a deeper disposition in me, despite my not having had a religious upbringing—and my passion for restoring old computers. These latter vintage objects, ensouled by time, history, and human creative effort, have taught me how much beauty and significance are embedded in things; they've taught me that things are like portals to entire wings in the palace of mind, whose vast and rich territory is otherwise inaccessible through mere thought. As a kid, I intuited this in my relationship with the one-eyed mountain and its cave of mysteries. As an adult, I know this to be the intuitive insight behind the Western love affair with matter, dysfunctional as the latter often becomes. We have the innate capacity to experience the material world as a cathedral of meaning and significance, the body of God. This is true even though, in our immaturity and confusion, we often lose ourselves in addictive and obsessive patterns of behavior— think of vain, materialistic, consumerist lifestyles—precisely because of our innate orientation to the material. Every blessing comes paired with a curse, and this is one of ours.

My time at CERN was the start of a whirlwind period of my life, in which I systematically pursued and achieved every goal in a list I had made, with the help of the Other, at the tender age of 14. Whilst still at CERN, I fell in love and got married. Next, I moved to the Netherlands—the first European country I had come to years earlier, and which I immediately, though strangely, recognized as home—with my then-wife, to pursue a career in the private sector. In parallel with my full-time work at the Philips Research Laboratories, I pursued and received my first PhD degree—in computer science and engineering— from the Eindhoven University of Technology. Although I experienced the first inkling of what one could call a mid-life crisis immediately thereafter, it was but fleeting so I ignored it; I was still too busy pursuing further goals in my list, such as starting a technology company. With two partners-in-crime I did precisely that in late 2002. The resulting reconfigurable computing start-up—Silicon Hive—would eventually be acquired by Intel in 2011. By late 2005, however, I had already moved to another major Dutch technology company, ASML, to pursue a corporate career, the next item in my list. And at 33 years of age—less than three years after having joined ASML—I was already promoted to senior management. I was the perfect embodiment of the Hero archetype: that which, like the Phoenix, rises from its own ashes and proceeds to overcome every challenge and difficulty, so to conquer the world. Then, I ran out of goals.

My list of life goals was the result of something the Other had whispered to me only two years after my father's passing: I was to die very early, in my mid-thirties, thus focus and clarity of purpose were of the essence. And because I felt equally attracted to multiple possible life-stories—scientist, tech entrepreneur, corporate executive, etc.—I couldn't compromise by excluding any. Therefore, I had to have laser-sharp attention and avoid wasting any time at all, so to be able to squeeze all those various paths into a very short life. As insane as this sounds to me today, it was perfectly reasonable to my younger self. But I would have been completely skeptical if someone, then, had told me what I know now: that all of it would be just a kind of prelude or preparation; that none of it was the real telos of my existence.

Psychologically, my list was an adaptive effort to squeeze meaning out of tragedy. My goals gave me clarity of direction and purpose. Pursuing them kept me busy, thus countering my brooding tendencies. More broadly speaking, however, my goals carved out a space in the world for me: achieving them granted me not only a respectable social position and relative economic comfort and means, but also gave me a podium to speak from as a philosopher, in a manner that people couldn't cavalierly dismiss. For I wasn't just a nut from the streets, but someone with respectable academic credentials and a history of relevant real-life successes.

I didn't know it then, but my list was a map to what Jung called "the first half of life," whose objective is to secure favorable conditions in society so one can, in the second half, pursue one's true purpose. The tragedy of the West is that, because we are so naturally inclined to, and skilled at, the ethos of the first half of life, we become over-specialized. When the game changes in the second half, we don't know what to do; our society doesn't give us the orientation, guidelines, and references for how to go about life at that point. Many of us then keep on playing the same game as in the first half—more money, more status, more power, more consumption—for they don't know how to do anything else. Others cannot help but realize that it's futile to pretend that what fulfilled them earlier, in the first half of life, can continue to do so in the second. These often fall prey to the dreaded mid-life crisis, characterized by depression, ennui, and complete loss of one's sense of direction. I belong in this latter group.

In the year I was promoted to senior management (in most companies, this means a vice-president position) I also bought the house of my dreams, shy of my thirty-fourth birthday. At that point, I thought I had arrived; I thought I had crossed the finish line in first place and it was finally time to uncork the champagne. I had overcome the tragedy of my youth and nothing could threaten me anymore. I felt I had achieved mastery over life and world, become untouchable, and that from that point on life would be one long, exhilarating celebration. I had completely forgotten the Other's whisper that I'd die early, in my mid-thirties. And so celebrate I did; for a few months at least.

Later that same year, I had a relatively minor confrontation with another senior manager at work; one of countless other instances of such routine confrontations that I had experienced throughout my career, without giving them a second thought. But this time, for some odd reason, it was different: the confrontation made clear to me that, relatively socially dominant as I had become, there is always someone more powerful. And although my first reaction was to conclude that I simply had to accrue yet more power, immediately the voice of the Other returned, after a long absence: "This is a never-ending game; if that's how you are going to live your life, you will never get to where you hope to be." That stopped me cold on my tracks. For the first time since I was 14 years old, I questioned my goals and direction. I intuitively knew—suddenly, then and there—that the game had fundamentally changed. Yet, it would take more to alter the course of my life, for old habits die hard; especially because they had been so effective at protecting me earlier. It's hard to mess with a hitherto winning recipe, even when it becomes clear that tastes have changed.

Nonetheless, life teaches; forcefully if need be. Not long after my otherwise minor and trite confrontation at work, I felt a lump in my then-wife's breast. It would take doctors two full weeks to determine that it was harmless. During that entire time—an almost endless, agonizing wait—I had to live with the possibility that something I was powerless to control could take a loved one away from me again. And that was a movie I didn't need to rewatch. I felt vulnerable again for the first time in many years. All my coping mechanisms entailed *undertaking action towards solutions*, so they went into reset when all I could do was to wait and hope. None of my hard-earned defensive weapons had any effect, for this wasn't a problem I could be on top of through sheer activity. Life had caught me entirely wrong-footed and I remembered the words of Nietzsche:

we must not ask the money-making banker the reason of his restless activity, it is foolish. The active roll as the stone rolls, according to the stupidity of mechanics.
(*Human, All Too Human*, translated by Helen Zimmern, T.N. Foulis, 1909, Section 283).

Since I was 14, I had rolled unthinkingly like the stone rolls— and now dropped like one too.

One would think that an educated 34-year-old should be mature enough to know the obvious fact that nobody can control the twists and turns of life. Yet, I clearly wasn't, for I sincerely believed that I could do precisely that, if only I worked hard enough for it. My entire sense of personal agency at that point—molded by how I survived my father's passing—relied precisely on this illusion of control, this imagined ability to preempt unwelcome surprises through sheer activity. And it all came crashing down, all at once, over my head.

What was already obvious to others suddenly became obvious to me too: I had no control over life; had never had and would never have. At best I could nudge it in certain directions, but certainly not take the reins of its course. All the adaptive mechanisms I had constructed to deal with loss, useful as they had been, had a fatal flaw: they deceived me into the illusion that I could amass enough power in life to prevent the rug from being pulled from under my feet again. Yet, there I was, dealing with the reality that the rug could indeed be pulled from under my feet again *at any time*, and there was nothing I or anyone else could do about it. Life had never been in my hands; all along, it was me who had always been in the hands of life, despite my delusions of control. I had never gotten to the place of safety I had desperately craved to reach since I was 12; that's not at all what my journey had been about. I hadn't arrived; at least not to the place I thought I had.

Again, one would think that two minor incidents—a routine confrontation at work and a health-related false alarm—couldn't fundamentally change anyone's outlook on life. And indeed, in and of themselves, they can't. But something else had been simmering within me all along; some silent inner process that had primed me for the major realization triggered by those two minor incidents. *Twenty years earlier the Other had laid a trap for me*; a bitter but benign trap that, just like my grand initiation to life upon my father's passing, would take me years to appreciate for the positive value it had.

Chapter 6

Enter the Daimon

One's first half of life is always seemingly about *oneself*. Your first half of life is or has been about *you*. My first half of life has been about *me*. This is so because we all must first carve out a space in the world for *ourselves*, so to ensure that we have food on the table, a roof over our heads, and enough resources to be able to express something new in the world. If one is constantly struggling with where one's next meal is going to come from, one cannot afford to spend time and energy on anything else. Moreover, if one has no resources beyond the minimum required for subsistence, one has little means to express oneself and serve a higher natural purpose. The basics must be dealt with first, so we have a podium from which to send our message to the world, as well as hear what the world has to say back to us.

Our entire culture provides us with tips and guidelines for dealing with this first half of life: we're told to get an education, a job, find a good partner, progress in our career, build a home, have kids, etc. Cruelly, for many people the need to fight for a place in the world never ends, and so they will never know how the game unexpectedly changes once one achieves the initial goals. But those of us who do succeed in carving out a minimal space for ourselves eventually face a wall, a dilemma: we ask ourselves, "what now?" Once you have the career, the home, the savings, the status and respect, what do you do with all that? What's next?

That was my dilemma. Upon suddenly becoming aware that I had never achieved any appreciable level of mastery over life and world—which is what had motivated me to pursue my journey in the first place—I wondered what all my struggles had been about. If growing so quickly in my career, accumulating savings and investments, achieving social status, and buying the house I wanted didn't give me the control and safety I craved, what did I do it all for? What was the point? And even more importantly: what to do *now*? What to live for from now on?

Once again, after 22 years, I had fallen into utter disorientation. All I knew was what *wouldn't* work: it wouldn't do to keep on playing the same game, for I never really cared about wealth beyond a minimum level of comfort to begin with. I didn't care about a second car, nicer clothing or shoes, let alone a yacht. I did care about control, but control of the kind I could accrue didn't solve or preempt the problems that mattered most to me, such as death and disease. So none of this would do. And I didn't know what, if anything, would.

That was my death; the death of the second, heroic Bernardo, the one who re-emerged from Hades armed to the teeth with adaptive, coping strategies that were entirely ineffective in the face of this new challenge: the second half of life. The Bernardo who thought he knew what life was about—the one who followed to the letter the cultural script for the first half of life—was now gone, dead, just like the Other had predicted two decades earlier; and with him, his entire view of life. The Other was right all along: I *did* die at 34.

My only consolation was that, since something in me—namely, the Other—knew from the beginning that this death was going to happen and yet kept on pushing me forward anyway, my struggles couldn't have been for nothing; my life hitherto couldn't have been just a mistake; instead, it had to have been a necessary phase or step towards something else that I couldn't yet discern, but which the Other in me, since very early on in the game, could. This faith in some vague inner knowledge was all I had left to keep going.

The death of the heroic Bernardo forced me to stop in my tracks and contemplate the big questions: what is life all about, given that what culture tells us proves entirely inadequate at some point? What is this thing we call a self, when there seem to be so many agencies within me, each with its own knowledge, dispositions, and will? What is this precarious, ephemeral process we call biology? What is its relationship with the rest of the Universe, such as quasars, blackholes, and supernovae? Where did we come from and where are we supposed to go? And what is the meaning of it all? Every time I attempted to return to the familiar, unexamined, reflexive way of living I had before, its utter untenability stopped me and forced me to contemplate these questions again and again. Life had decided that a different path—namely, philosophy—had to be followed, and who was I to argue against it?

Yet, it is exquisitely hard to let go of adaptive, autonomous habits and reflexes, even after they prove inadequate. I held on to things for as long as I could: career, relationship, behaviors, the lot. I didn't know how else to go about life. But I did notice that the world started conspiring against my insistence on playing the same game. Things that once came easily and naturally became hard and laborious. Doors that would once open automatically had to be effectively kicked down. Opportunities that were once plentiful dried up. When one is on the wrong path, the world seems to rearrange itself to make progress difficult, if at all possible. And so it was that, over the next few years, my career growth would grind to a halt, my marriage would come to an end, and even a dear pet would pass away before her time, as if to force a clean break with the past. I resisted all this, but the flow of life is brutal and unstoppable; it goes where it wants to go—carrying us along—not to where we are rowing. By forcibly dragging me with it, life betrayed me for a second time.

In the thick of this process, the following words came to me one morning, before I could even step out of bed:

I grieve the loss of my innocence.
The mystery and possibilities that once were my world abandoned me,
Frivolousness and claustrophobia left in their stead.

Each door traversed turned an infinitude of magical could-be's into one cold has-been.
No longer an endless, multi-dimensional path ahead,
But a long line of footprints behind.

I ache in sorrow not for my failures, but for my successes.
They revealed the hollowness of early dreams,
Failing my childhood.

I feel grievously disappointed in people,
From whom I once expected wisdom, strength and reassurance,
But who are just as lost as me.

Knowledge betrayed me.
Maturity is the fall, and I fell.
Having seen through my innocence, I now feel naked and vulnerable.

In knowing, I have come to distrust the world.
Even my own body is an insidious alien forced upon me by nature,
Ready to ambush me at any time.

I feel angry at nature for her being what she is.
I feel furious at myself for having been such a fool,
And for having allowed myself to drift so far from where I started.

There are no masters.
There is no safe refuge.

There is nothing to hold on to.

Where did I lose myself?
When?
Why?

Fragments of shattered dreams,
Evanescent shadows of what I once was,
Are all I still have.

I desperately miss the myth that once was real.

Re-reading these words now, I am sucked right back into that dark space, my second visit to Hades, which would cost me well over a decade to fully re-emerge from.

As hinted at by some of the verses above, the main way life forced its direction on me was by exploiting my newly rediscovered sense of powerlessness. What was originally an awareness that fatal illness could take a loved one away from me again became internalized, leading to my own health anxieties: fatal illness could affect *me too*; I had no mastery *even over my own body*. Yes, I could nudge my health in the right direction and influence the odds but, ultimately, anyone can—and will—be struck down and there is nothing one can do about it. I suppose everyone knows this at least conceptually, but *I really knew it*; to me it was a felt, lived reality that began to overwhelm me every time I tried to get on with my regular life. The dread of what my body could be covertly engendering out of my sight turned into sheer torture. Every moment became the throw of life-or-death dice, a Russian roulette. And I was exquisitely good at torturing myself this way; for, as Nietzsche once wrote, "nature has outfitted me terribly well to be a self-tormentor! ... my imagination [is] stronger than my reason" (*Selected Letters of Friedrich Nietzsche*, edited and translated by Christopher

Middleton, Hackett Publishing Company Inc., 1996, page 209). This runaway, self-imposed anxiety made my world small, neurotic, and fear ridden; it made it impossible for me to rely — as I had done for the previous 22 years — on any sense of control to feel safe; it brutally forced me to find another way to be.

Over time, I began to notice that the anxiety would only let go when I made time and mental space to contemplate the big questions and then write my thoughts down. There was something about allowing philosophy to flow through me, and then articulating it in written words, that kept the discomfort at bay. As a matter of fact, occasionally the anxiety would become so crippling that *the only thing I could do was to write philosophy*; it was uncanny. This is how my first ten books came into being: each and every one of them was relentlessly forced upon me at great personal cost.

I have many shortcomings, but lack of thoughtfulness has never been one. So I quickly took notice of the pattern at play here: something — some agency — in me wanted me to philosophize and write. Could it be the Other? Perhaps. But if so, he had changed: earlier, he didn't seem to have an agenda of his own. As a kid, for instance, I wanted to stop suffering after the death of my father, and the Other helped me achieve just that. He would always help me achieve *my* goals, not his own. However, becoming a professional philosopher had never been my goal, despite my innate predisposition to philosophizing. I had never desired to become a published author either. Instead, all I had always wanted was to find things out and then build cool stuff with that knowledge, as engineers do. If it was the Other — i.e., the same internal, semi-dissociated psychic complex I had experienced as a kid — who was forcing me down this new philosophical path, then he had developed an agenda of his own now; he no longer cared about *my* — i.e., my ego's — goals. Moreover, earlier the Other only observed, advised, reassured, but never *forced* me to do anything. And now, whatever in me was causing my anxiety, was downright coercing me to pursue its philosophical goals.

Amazingly, the world seemed to respond to this new, impersonal agenda. Publishing my first book was surprisingly easy. And even my next two or three books were also taken up by my publisher before I had achieved any significant level of visibility and recognition as an author. Moreover, established authors and media personalities spontaneously offered me their help, opened doors for me, even though I was a nobody in this field so new to me. Yes, I understood that they saw value in what I had to say, but there is so much value in what so many other people have to say that I couldn't fathom this being the only reason why they were extending their hand to me; why not to a million other struggling authors with important ideas? Just as my corporate career seemed to become increasingly difficult, my new career as a philosopher and author seemed to acquire a momentum of its own. The world seemed to want me to speak philosophy, just as much as the Other in me did; so much so that world and Other no longer seemed to be different entities. Instead, they merged into one and the same agency.

It would take me years to realize that what, in the first half of life, comes across to us as the benign, observing Other, in the second half begins to forcefully impose its own agenda on a Western mind. In both cases, we are talking about the same impersonal force within; the only difference is that, in the first half of life, its agenda *happens* to line up with ours—because it knows that we must first carve out a space in the world for ourselves, if we are to be useful and effective instruments of its expression later on—while in the second half it doesn't. At all times, however, this impersonal force within is always only following *its own agenda*. To highlight the distinctly impersonal character of its behavior in the second half of life, I shall henceforth call this force the *Daimon* and refer to it as an "it," instead of a "he."

The Daimon is just nature as it expresses itself in us and through us. And nature is, of course, impersonal. Its agenda is universal and holistic, not restricted to the petty egoic tastes and preferences of a person. It is naïve to expect a human being to be able to comprehend the Daimon's universal agenda, just as it is naïve to expect an apple blossom to comprehend what its role is in the grand scheme of apple trees and life on Earth. We are segments of nature, not mere witnesses; we didn't parachute into nature, but grew out of it. Therefore, *we are nature*, as expressed in a particular volume of spacetime. Given this, it is also naïve to expect there to be no impersonal force—no impersonal *will*—acting within us, and through us; of course there is. And I call it the Daimon.

Many of the characteristic dispositions of the Western mind that I discussed earlier simply reflect the presence of the Daimon within. The teleological arch of our lives—our need to live for a purpose—is a felt, though implicit, acknowledgment of the primacy of the Daimon's agenda as the driver of, and reason for, life. Indeed, our felt need for a purpose is the intuitive passion that links us to the Daimon's impersonal will. The idiosyncrasies of our individuality, too, reflect the particular expression of the Daimon in each of us. We are individuals only insofar as the Daimon's will in us is differentiated. Our Western love affair with matter also reflects the Daimon's unabashed interest in realizing its impersonal agenda through engagement with the world, not detachment from it. We love matter because the Daimon in us wants to express itself in the world. Finally, the tremendous creative—and sometimes destructive—energies mobilized by the Western mind are the formidable power of the Daimon, an explosive force of nature akin to a tornado, volcano, or tsunami. The Great Goethe spoke of it ominously:

the most fearful manifestation of the Daimonical is when it is seen predominating in some individual character.... a tremendous energy seems to be seated in [such persons], and they exercise a wonderful power over all creatures, and even over the elements; and, indeed, who shall say how much farther such influence may extend?

(Johan Wolfgang von Goethe, *The Autobiography of Goethe: Truth and Poetry: From My Own Life*, translated by John Oxenford, Books I–XX, Revised Edition, George Bell and Sons, 1897, page 679)

Ultimately, a Western life is always about the Daimon within. Stronger yet, beneath the veneer of personhood, a Western life *is* the life of the Daimon, not that of the person. This has been made potently clear by the Daimon's own voice, which Richard Buckminster Fuller heard as he was about to commit suicide:

You do not have the right to eliminate yourself. You do not belong to you. You belong to the Universe. Your significance will remain forever obscure to you, but you may assume that you are fulfilling your role if you apply yourself to converting your experiences to the highest advantage of others.

(Lloyd Steven Sieden, *Buckminster Fuller's Universe: His Life and Work*, Basic Books, 1989, pages 87–88)

The Daimon has been an ever-present figure in the Western philosophical, artistic, and scientific traditions, and arguably responsible for their very inceptions. Already in the last chapter of Plato's *Republic*, the Daimon's existence and role are explicitly laid out in the Myth of Er. Socrates, too, spoke extensively of his Daimon: an inner voice that would warn him every time he was about to take a wrong turn or make the wrong decision. It was the absence of this voice at his trial that reassured Socrates of forfeiting his self-defense, even though such inaction would lead to his execution by poisoning. René Descartes spoke of a vision he had in the winter of 1619 to 1620, where his Daimon—in the form of a divine spirit—told him that the keys to understanding nature were number and measure. This seminal idea would go on to form the basis of Western science. Indeed, the very fabric of Western thought and life is Daimonic.

When the Daimon compels us to follow its agenda through seduction—i.e., by "pulling from the front," like the proverbial carrot—we tend to call it the Muse, Genius, the Siren Song, or—more prosaically—Inspiration, which artists have spoken of through the ages. When it forces its agenda through coercion—i.e., by "pushing from behind," like the proverbial stick—we tend to regard it as a negative, even tyrannic force, for—as Buckminster Fuller's Daimon made clear—we lack the breadth of awareness to comprehend the broad natural context that gives Daimonic lives their meaning. Nietzsche wrote of his pushing Daimon:

> I have an *aim*, which compels me to go on living and for the sake of which I *must* cope with even the most painful matters.... the "tyrant in me," the inexorable tyrant, *wills* that I conquer this time too.
>
> (*Selected Letters of Friedrich Nietzsche*, edited and translated by Christopher Middleton, Hackett, 1996, page 214, original emphasis)

And:

> that *passion*, to which no name can be put for a long time, rescues us from all digressions and dispersions, that *task* of which one is the involuntary missionary.
>
> (*Ibid.*, page 281, original emphasis)

In more recent times, psychologist James Hillman spoke of the Daimon—in his so-called "acorn theory" of personality—variously as the Soul, Calling, or Vocation. The idea is that there lies within each person a latent blueprint of their unique character and destiny, much like an acorn embodies the potential to become a particular oak tree. Hillman argued that our individuality and purpose are innate, not contingent. The defining agency behind this innateness is the Daimon, which orients our lives mainly through "hints, intuitions, whispers, and the sudden urges and oddities that disturb your life and that we continue to call symptoms" (*The Soul's Code*, Bantam Books, 1996, page 10).

Many have written compellingly about the Daimon in the Western tradition. Recapitulating more of that material in a scholarly fashion is beyond the aims and style of this little book. For those interested in further reading, I generally recommend the extraordinary corpus of Patrick Harpur, one of the most criminally underrated scholars of our time. Here, instead, I'll continue to leverage my own personal experiences to highlight the role of the Daimon in the Western mind.

Without the forceful—even brutal—intervention of the Daimon, I would almost certainly have continued to roll mechanically like a stone, to live an unexamined life; a myopic life about myself, not about nature as a whole. The suffering it imposed on me was the seed of almost everything that will come to be regarded as my legacy, for, as James Hollis observed,

Consciousness only comes from suffering; without some form of suffering—physical, emotional, spiritual—we are content to rest easy in the old dispensations, the old comforts, the old dependencies.
(*Under Saturn's Shadow: The Wounding and Healing of Men*, Inner City Books, 1994, page 19)

Schopenhauer saw this too:

> Unless suffering is the direct and immediate object of life,
> our existence must entirely fail of its aim. It is absurd to
> look upon the enormous amount of pain that abounds
> everywhere in the world, and originates in needs and
> necessities inseparable from life itself, as serving no
> purpose at all and the result of mere chance.
>
> (*Arthur Schopenhauer: Essays and Aphorisms*, Translated
> by R. J. Hollingdale, Penguin Books, 1970, page 41)

It's not suffering itself that is the telos of life, but what it
brings about and then sustains. Life is what happens around
the backbone of suffering, even though we often miss it for the
suffering itself—we think that we are only suffering, when the
flesh of life is what is unfolding around it.

Agony and travail are not only the engines of insight, but
also the seeds of great—perhaps even the *greatest*—beauty, such
as Nietzsche's *Thus Spoke Zarathustra* (written after the defining
heartbreak of Friedrich's life: his rejection by Lou Salomé),
Mozart's *Requiem* (composed as Wolfgang lay dying), van
Gogh's *The Starry Night* (painted while Vincent was interned
in a lunatic asylum, suffering from intense emotional distress),
and James's *Moving On* (composed upon the deaths of Tim
Booth's mother and best friend).

My own Daimonic suffering—my Daimon is of the kind
that uses the stick, not the carrot—jolted me out of a sleepy
local minimum and propelled my life forward in the direction
of its true telos. Nature does not have patience to wait for
us to catch up with it, to *understand* where we are supposed
to go; life is too short for this kind of indulgence, so we must
be pushed forward, kicking and screaming if need be. And I
was consistently pushed, kicking and screaming, towards
confronting the big philosophical questions. My Daimon was

assertive to the point of near sadism, and today I am thankful to it for that; for I now understand that, given how strong I can be in resisting the inevitable, there was no other way. I had to be beaten into submission, and dully was.

Earlier in life, I had been allowed to achieve my adolescent list of personal ambitions only so that, later, I would have both the emotional space and the mundane resources to allow nature to do through me what nature—not me—wants. And this is the great discovery of the second half of life: *our life isn't, has never been, and can't ever be about us.* That the first half of life is focused on our personal goals is merely a necessary step in the direction of the impersonal, for we can only be effective instruments of nature's self-expression when we have carved out a space in the world for ourselves. The first half of life is about crafting and polishing the instrument, while the second is about allowing nature to play the instrument the way nature wishes to.

This metaphor was shared with me by my dear friend Fred Matser, founder of Essentia Foundation and the visionary behind it, as well as one of the most influential figures in my life: "we must allow ourselves to be played" by nature, he said, "like a violin allows itself to be played by the musician." Persisting with an egoic, personal agenda into the second half of life is akin to sticking chewing gum to the strings of the violin: the whole thing goes out of tune. To offer strong resistance to the Daimon increases suffering beyond need and derails life, making the music dissonant. Fred saw this early in his own life. He also saw it in *my* life long before I did, thereby turning himself into an instrument of my Daimon, just as much as I probably am an instrument of his.

One of the cruelest ironies of Western life is that, today, the key, unquestioned, seemingly self-evident axiom of the Western wellbeing and self-help industry is precisely that our life is about *us*; that we have to wrestle the reins of our life from mere happenstance and circumstance and determine its course ourselves; that we have to proactively pursue *our* agenda and project meaning onto it; and—perhaps cruelest of all—that our life is about *our being happy*. All of this is unnatural and unjustified to the point of being grotesque. One can only take this preposterous, in-your-face nonsense seriously if one hasn't given it 30 seconds of critical thought. Is the life of an apple blossom about the apple blossom? If not, then for precisely the same reason ours cannot be about us. Why would it? We are part of nature; why would our life be about us and not nature as a whole?

To add insult to injury, the outrageous view that our life is about our happiness lays on our shoulders a weight of responsibility no human—no living creature—could ever hope to bear. We aren't Atlas. There are many more variables with a direct bearing on our ability to be happy than we could ever hope to catalogue, let alone control. *We can't make ourselves happy*; it is as impossible as it is unnatural. We may experience flashes of happiness if the impersonal flow of nature happens to momentarily bring us to a happy place—in which case the only appropriate response is gratitude, for this is a form of natural Grace—but we can't force it, win it, earn it, or determine it, any more than an apple blossom can force the apple tree to keep it forever open and fresh. But since the culture of the *Letzter Mensch*—who "have invented happiness"—tells us that this insufferable, Atlantean task is what our life is all about, we keep on trying and failing, thereby making life frustrating by construction. It's a complete catch-22, a blind alley, a guarantee that we will make ourselves more miserable than we need to be.

The day I understood that my life hadn't been, wasn't, and would never be about me—let alone my personal happiness—but about the Daimon's agenda instead, was both a life-sentence and a great liberation. A life-sentence because I understood that Bernardo Kastrup is an instrument—a means to a natural end I could never even hope to fathom—not a separate agent with his own agenda; Bernardo Kastrup is a slave to the Daimon, therein residing the very meaning and glory of his life. A liberation because the exceptionally oppressive responsibility of controlling my life and making myself happy—impossible and unnatural tasks—was lifted off my shoulders in one fell swoop, allowing me to finally straighten my back and live with dignity. What a freeing breath of fresh air it was, as if the windows of a dark, damp bedroom had been opened anew to the young, cool breeze of early dawn.

From the vantage point I occupy today, I cannot begin to describe to you how ludicrous the idea seems to me that we are the masters of our lives, arbiters of fate, and dispensers of meaning; it's like the apple blossom proclaiming itself king of the tree, and just as laughable. Our culture is caught up in a Promethean complex that is preventing us from relating to life in a natural way; it borders on a collective psychosis that I, too, have been a victim of for most of my life.

If you can see things the way they actually are, you will be a truly free Western mind forever enslaved to your Daimon. For you will then realize that *you are not directly responsible for outcomes*; the only thing you are directly responsible for is to play your natural part in the novel—or better yet, to allow nature to play you the way it wants. That's it; that's the sum-total of your onus. What will then unfold at the macroscales of family, work, society, culture, world, and cosmos *is not your direct responsibility*—it's nature's, the Daimon's. And your happiness isn't your responsibility either. It isn't even a goal in and of itself, but a fortuitous side-effect of some of life's motions. Why would nature care if your whimsical egoic agenda is being accomplished or not? As a matter of fact, why should *you* care? *It's not about you*; it has never been and will never be. Drop this Promethean weight off your shoulders and be free again, as nature made you.

If you aren't feeling happy, it's alright; this is not unnatural; you are not inadequate or a failure; and neither do you have to change it. You don't have the obligation or duty to be happy. Insofar as your suffering is natural—as opposed to self-imposed in an unnecessary, pathological manner—it is not something to be rejected, fought against, repressed, or pushed away. It's not your natural goal to get rid of your suffering, for the latter is often nature's tool to steer you in the right direction and compel you to look deeper. Painful events "perhaps are the only ways the gods can wake us up," wrote Hillman (*The Soul's Code*, Bantam Books, 1996, page 278). The adequate reaction to suffering is *to pay attention to it critically*, for your suffering—unless, again, it is self-imposed in an artificial manner—is trying to show you something, propel you towards something, force some creative act out of you. Suffering is the Daimon's tool to prevent you from getting stuck and steer you in the direction nature has in mind for you. This is the fate of the Western mind: to pursue its natural teleological arch propelled by Daimonic suffering. This is what the Native American elder who spoke to Jung saw in our eyes. It is scary and poignant, no doubt; but also wonderful and powerful.

Make no mistake: the Bernardo Kastrup you know is almost entirely Daimonic, a creation of the impersonal within me. It is the Daimon that is writing this book—even though I do get to choose the particular words used, which is my service to the Daimon—as it now seems to want to take the credit it has been due. Before my thirty-fifth year, I had never anticipated or wished for this philosophy gig I've been performing, and to this day it feels somewhat alien. This, in fact, is the reason for my well-known dubious relationship with big media: next to my being a natural introvert, part of me still resists achieving great visibility for something I don't quite identify with. As a matter of fact, most of the interviews I give are secretly selected and (mis) used by me as exercises to refine my wording of philosophical ideas, not actually to project my image as a philosopher; for I know that that is not what the kid in me is. What I *really* am is hardly ever visible publicly: I am a 1970s kid who likes to tinker with computers and hike in the mountains; that's it; that's all I have been my whole life, to this day. And it took me 46 years to realize it. Everything else is the Daimon.

Which, of course, raises the question: *how do I know all this?* How do I know what is me and what is another agency within me? How do I distinguish the Daimon's agenda from my own? How do I know that the whole Daimon thing isn't just my secret ego-protection mechanisms at play, or a wish-fulfilling fantasy?

In the beginning, it wasn't easy to figure this out. For the longest time I was riddled with doubt, persistently thinking of the Daimon as a convenient fantasy—a self-deception— meant to reduce my suffering, conjure up meaning, or evade moral responsibility. You see, what makes it so difficult to pin the Daimon down is that—at least in my case—it isn't like a character of a dream or hallucination, perceivable to us only insofar as its external, imagined appearance is concerned; it isn't someone we talk to or shake hands with in our imagination. Instead, it is part of our own first-person, subjective perspective. I know of the Daimon's presence in me only because *I think its thoughts, feel its feelings, and want its wants,* just as I experience my own thoughts, feelings, and will. This, right there, is what complicates the whole affair. For if I experience the Daimon's thoughts, feelings, and will just as I experience my own, how do I know which ones are mine and which aren't?

Despite these doubts, I could never shake off the felt presence of the Daimon. It is sticky and relentless. There is something persuasive about it that betrays its alienness. Think of it as if you could telepathically connect to another human being—one very different from you in character and dispositions. This telepathic link would allow you to experience their thoughts, feelings, and wants directly, just as you experience your own. Yet, you would definitely know that those particular thoughts, feelings, and wants aren't yours, wouldn't you? You wouldn't recognize them as your own because they wouldn't fit with everything else you know about yourself. You would say to yourself: "this stuff isn't mine!" even though you would be experiencing it from a first-person perspective. Such inability to identify with some of our own mental contents is precisely what betrays the impersonal Daimonic presence within.

It took me years to discern the boundaries, the contours of the Daimon in my own field of subjectivity. Only laboriously did I begin to introspectively grasp, with great difficulty at first, the exquisite, multi-layered subtleties and nuances of the movements of the impersonal within. But today, I am comfortable to say that I largely know what in me is Daimonic, and what isn't. The Daimon has been with me long and intensely enough that I can now recognize it clearly. Nonetheless, because this recognition is mostly intuitive and ineffable—much like a smell, vague and furtive, though unmistakably there—I can't provide a surefire recipe for you to recognize your own Daimon in yourself. Like much in the Western mind, the character of the Daimon's presence, too, is uniquely individual.

What I *can* share with you, though in frustratingly vague and general terms, are some of the typical signs of the Daimonic in our inner lives, the shapes of the footprints it leaves behind in our minds.

The first sign is how impersonal the Daimon feels: it couldn't care less about our safety or comfort; it doesn't care whether we will have food on the table tomorrow or be able to pay for health insurance next month. It disregards the reasonable demands and expectations the social contract places upon us. In this particular sense, it is brutal and uncaring, and can easily be mistaken for a self-destructive impulse. Nonetheless, the Daimon is *not* destructive towards us, for it needs us to express itself. It's just that, like any force of nature—think of a volcanic eruption, or a tornado—it isn't reflective, discerning, or thoughtful, but instead instinctive and spontaneous. It is way too absorbed into its own teleological arch to pay any attention to the care of its instrument. This is why *we must always look out for ourselves while giving expression to the impersonal in us.*

Although we cannot bargain with the Daimon, we *can* reason with it. In my case, it goes something like this: "I see you. I recognize your existence and your nature-given right to use me as your instrument. I know what you want and fully intend to do your bidding. But in order to do so, I must make sure that I have the capabilities and resources necessary to act on your behalf. For this reason, I can't just blindly follow your prodding; I must take care of my immediate needs too, so I can more effectively work towards your goals. If I don't do so, we both lose. So please be patient and bear with me. It is in *your* best interest to do so." This inner attitude towards the Daimon—reverential but also assertive, like that of Job talking to God—often works for me.

Besides reasoning with the Daimon on our own behalf, we also carry the moral responsibility to oversee our Daimonic impulses when it comes to their potential effects on others and the world at large. Allow me to belabor this point, for it is of crucial importance: *we cannot allow the Daimon—the impersonal force within us—to run amok;* we admittedly must give it space to act in the world, *but always under moral supervision.* By this I mean that we must exercise and pass ethical judgment on every Daimonic impulse before acting on it. The Daimon, as a spontaneous force of nature devoid of the higher-level mental functions present in the human ego, cannot do so itself.

Beyond knowing which mouth to bring the fork to, this is thus the ego's function: moral oversight. An unsupervised Daimon can be destructive to the level of a civilization-ending catastrophe. As I write these words, Vladimir Putin—leveraging the Daimonic force he has naively and unthinkingly co-opted, hence tragically coming to believe that the Daimon in him *is him*—threatens to push the nuclear button. Hitler, too, allowed his Daimon—driven by the impulse to restore dignity to the German peoples—to run amok. We all know how that went down. When the ego uncritically co-opts Daimonic forces without moral discernment, great perils are constellated. Just as volcanoes and tornados are indiscriminate in their action, so is an unsupervised or ego-co-opted Daimon. The Great Goethe warned of this danger already two centuries ago:

> Although this Daimonic element can manifest itself in all corporeal and incorporeal things,... with man, especially does it stand in a most wonderful connexion, forming in him a power which, if it be not opposed to the moral order of the world, nevertheless does often so cross it that one may be regarded as the warp, and the other as the woof.... All the moral powers combined are of no avail against [Daimonic egos]; in vain does the more enlightened portion of mankind attempt to throw suspicion upon them as deceived if not deceivers—the mass is still drawn on by them.
>
> (*The Autobiography of Goethe: Truth and Poetry: From My Own Life*, translated by John Oxenford, Books I–XX, Revised Edition, London, George Bell and Sons, 1897, page 679)

Although I do believe that "all the moral powers combined" *can* deter otherwise unmitigated and potentially evil, ego-co-opted Daimonic expression, we would do well to heed Goethe's warning. Circling back to a point I endeavored to highlight earlier, to secure the moral boundaries of our own Daimonic expression *we must explicitly understand evil*; we must understand how evil rides the formidable energy of the Daimon, so we can recognize its ways and stop the process in time. The power of the Daimon—just like that of a volcano, a tornado, or any other spontaneous force of nature—is morally neutral, even ambivalent, and can thus be directed towards nefarious actions.

Crucial to our ability to supervise the Daimon, and thereby deter evil, is *to always think of it as a separate agency*. Jung emphasized this as a useful maneuver to help us retain moral ground. Co-opting the Daimon at the level of the ego can be catastrophic, as the ego becomes blind to whatever it co-opts, for the same reason that we become blind to whatever is just under our nose. We can't see what is too close. An ego that has co-opted the Daimon—thereby thinking of itself *as* the Daimon—cannot see or supervise it. It thus becomes vulnerable, for "what we do not know, controls us" (James Hollis, *Under Saturn's Shadow*, Inner City Books, 1994, page 29). Indeed, Daimonic co-option leads to ego-inflation of cataclysmic proportions; it can make a person think of themselves as a whole people and literally destroy the world. It is thus crucial that we maintain a healthy separation between our meta-cognitive ego and the instinctive movements of the impersonal within us. We must regard the latter as external, objective, and therefore amenable to supervision, checks and balances. This is why, in my own life, I've made the deliberate choice *to always speak of the Daimon in the third person*, even when I am speaking of it to myself, in my own inner chatter. As far as ordinary, daily activity is concerned, I am *not* my Daimon.

Another frequent characteristic of the Daimonic impulse is that it doesn't explain itself to us. Instead, "it disturbs the heart, it bursts out in temper,... It excites, calls, demands—but rarely does it offer a grand purpose," wrote Hillman (*The Soul's Code*, Bantam Books, 1996, page 197). This is so because the Daimon can't explain itself *even to itself*, let alone to us. As a force of nature, its sense of teleological direction is spontaneous, instinctive, reflexive, not the result of deliberate, narrative-based planning. Therefore, when driven by the Daimon we often cannot account for *why* we feel compelled to do, or not do, certain things; we don't comprehend how our actions fit into an overarching story or purpose. Yet, such a lack of understanding doesn't deter us at all. This peculiarity is, in fact, one of the most distinguishing signs of the stirrings of the impersonal within us. When it is personal goals or agendas that motivate our actions, we always have a neat, coherent story to account for them, to tell ourselves *why* we should do this, that, or the other thing. This explanatory story betrays the presence of egoic deliberations and machinations. The impersonal, in turn, provides no such story; it wouldn't bother to explain itself to us even if it could. When asked about the reasons for their actions or wishes, people moved by the Daimon will often say: "*I just know* that this is what I must do."

Our inability to tell ourselves and others the "why" behind our Daimonic life-choices can be both psychologically trying and socially alienating. Strong faith in often vague intuition is required to stay the course in the absence of a sensible, reassuring, explicit rationale to justify our choices and actions. Other people—such as friends and family—also won't understand why we aren't pursuing more reasonable life-paths, since we ourselves can't make intellectual sense of our choices either. That we just know what we must do, regardless of rationale, is typical of a Western Daimonic orientation.

I confess to have faced this dilemma many times. For instance, more than once have I found myself unwilling to pursue certain promising avenues of promotion for my philosophy work, without understanding why. All sensible lines of reasoning encouraged me strongly to pursue those avenues and reach more people—everyone who writes a book wants to reach people—yet something in me refused to do so. Other times, I felt compelled to do certain interviews, events, or pieces of writing that, at face value, didn't fit into any coherent narrative for progressing my life. You see, the Daimon always adopts the long view, because it always operates *sub specie aeternitatis*. This long view spans much more than a human lifetime and unfolds along multi-layered webs of causation that far exceed the ability of the human intellect to grasp. *We can't know why the Daimon wants to pursue certain things and refuses to engage in others;* its long view cannot be corralled into the pedestrian confines of human conceptual models and narratives. All we can do is trust the inner whispers, under moral oversight.

Allow me to give you a concrete historical example—akin to what I confessed above—to illustrate this point. Although he deeply craved to reach his contemporaries through his writing, Nietzsche never rationalized—let alone pursued—explicit ways to do so. Instead, he remained instinctively committed to the Daimonic orientation in him. He wrote what he felt had to be written, *sub specie aeternitatis*, despite knowing that his contemporaries couldn't relate to his material. "I live as if the centuries were nothing, and I pursue my thoughts without thinking of the date and of the newspapers," he wrote to his friend Franz Overbeck in November of 1880 (*Selected Letters of Friedrich Nietzsche*, edited and translated by Christopher Middleton, Hackett, 1996, page 174). If you were to ask him why this contradiction—or at least misalignment—between his wishes and actions, I strongly suspect he wouldn't be able to explain himself to you.

In the early 1870s, when Nietzsche was just starting his writing career, one of the most popular and well-known authors in Germany was theologian David Strauss. His defining book, *The Life of Jesus Critically Examined*, went through several editions and reprints during Nietzsche's lifetime, and sold a huge number of copies for nineteenth-century standards. However, the way Strauss achieved this success was so antithetical to Nietzsche's Daimonic values that it provoked a scathing public response by him, rumored to have contributed to Strauss's death shortly thereafter. In an essay titled "David Strauss: the Confessor and the Writer," part of Nietzsche's second book, *Untimely Meditations*, Nietzsche took exception to what he regarded as Strauss's mediocre writing and deliberate pandering to popular tastes and prejudices, for the sake of selling his book. In other words, Nietzsche was accusing Strauss of taking the short view, focused on personal gain, as opposed to the Daimonic purity of spirit Nietzsche himself was soon going to embody.

At the time, one could easily have accused Nietzsche of petty envy, since Strauss was a vastly more successful author. But Nietzsche's Daimon operated under the long view. And because of that, today you know who Nietzsche was and are even likely to be able to list some of his main ideas—the Eternal Return, the *Übermensch* and the *Letzter Mensch, Amor Fati* (love of fate), Master and Slave Morality, etc.—for the man has literally changed the world. But had you ever heard of David Strauss before reading the above? This is the nature of the Daimonic impulse: it disregards immediate and short-term outcomes, for it knows what we can't know, so to secure its teleological arch in the long run. If you were an author, whose ultimate fate would you rather have: that of Strauss, or that of Nietzsche?

Nietzsche spent much of his time as a traveling hermit, going from guesthouse to guesthouse across Germany, Switzerland, and northern Italy, never promoting his work. He ostensibly expected his publisher to do so, although he knew it never happened. In his delightfully sarcastic autobiography titled *Ecce Homo*—in which, incidentally, he conflates his books with his life, in an unmistakably Daimonic lapse—he claims that he knew the names of everyone who had read his books, because he had given them the books himself! He then bitterly admits, in one of the most poignant passages of his entire corpus, that "I live on my own self-made credit, and it is probably only a prejudice to suppose that I am alive at all" (Anthony

M. Ludovici translation, T.N. Foulis, 1911, page 1). Nietzsche never knew philosophical fame, only neglect, rejection, and isolation. Yet, his Daimon did know his ultimate lot: "I know my destiny. There will come a day when my name will recall the memory of something formidable" (*Ibid.*, page 131). In a letter to Nietzsche's mother, written in October of 1887, his Daimon wrote prophetically:

> I am well enough acquainted with human nature to know how the judgment on me will have been reversed in fifty years' time, and with what a splendor of reverence your son's name will then shine, on account of the same things as those for which I have till now been mishandled and abused.
>
> (*Selected Letters of Friedrich Nietzsche*, edited and translated by Christopher Middleton, Hackett Publishing Company Inc., 1996, page 271)

Nietzsche, through his Daimon Zarathustra, acted under the long view. He didn't know any of the "why's" for his actions and inactions. He achieved no recognition during his sane lifetime, and thus never had any reassurance at all that he was on the right path. Yet, he is now recognized as the most influential philosopher of all time, even above Plato himself. Nietzsche didn't do what he did because he understood how his actions were building up to some grand purpose; he simply trusted his Daimon, which never explained itself to him. Daimons never do.

The third telltale sign of Daimonic presence is that it always pushes towards something that, though not necessarily part of one's personal agenda, one happens to be good at. Nature is not inconsistent: it chooses its instruments wisely; it won't expect of one something one can't do; it will make sure one has the gift—the skillset—required to pursue one's fate. So if you think it's the Daimon forcing you to do something you not only don't wish to, but also *can't* do, then think twice: instead of the Daimon, the push may be coming from some secret self-deceptive narrative of your own.

The cruel thing about this Daimonic dynamic is that what one is good at isn't necessarily what gives one pleasure; it isn't necessarily what one wants for oneself. Nature's gifts, if contemplated from a purely egoic perspective, are also curses. This very book is a case in point: I take no pleasure in writing it; I experience my writing it as a responsibility, a duty, a heavy load, a cross to be carried. The same applies to all my previous books as well. Indeed, I have never written a single philosophy book, essay, or paper that I simply wanted to write, because doing so was fun—it wasn't, not ever. What I really want to do with my personal time is hike in the mountains, tinker with computers, and spend time with my partner and pets. Doing philosophy does give me a sense of purpose—of meaning—but not of pleasure or personal gratification.

Nonetheless, I can write philosophy books with relative ease: the understanding underlying them comes effortlessly to me, without being prompted, whether I want it or not; I just can't stop the flow. Moreover, I recognize that I am relatively good at finding the words to express this continuous flow of understanding. This is my curse: precisely *because* I seem to be in a relatively privileged position to express the stuff that comes to me, I have an overwhelming, oppressive sense of responsibility for doing so. Yet I don't *like* it. The only pleasant part of the job is the relief—and release—of finally completing it and being done with the whole thing; that is, until the next understanding demanding to be expressed knocks at the door of my mind. "Oh shit, here we go again," I mutter to myself in quiet despair. Being good at what I am doing right now, as I write these words, is the very chain that binds me to my Daimon; it is the tool of my subjugation to the flow of the impersonal within me.

This brings me to the fourth telltale sign of the Daimon's presence: a sense of destiny, related to the feeling of duty and responsibility discussed above. If you feel that you can *easily* give up on what you are doing and choose to do something completely else with your life, then you aren't performing the archetypal work that constitutes your fate. For fate has a momentum—a compelling, almost irresistible inertia—to it. When one finds oneself walking the path of one's Daimonic lot, stopping or changing course becomes as difficult and laborious as turning the Titanic away from the proverbial iceberg. The ease of exercising one's natural gifts and the world's receptiveness—even acquiescence—to one's actions conspire to maintain one's course. And if one nonetheless insists on the wrong path, the sense of guilt—of wasted time and opportunity, even of wasted life, and of failing one's calling—quickly sets in and overwhelms one. The Daimon can be ruthless in this regard.

On the positive side, doing the Daimon's bidding—i.e., accepting one's natural fate—saturates life with meaning. They who are fulfilling their fates never experience nihilism, or lose touch with life's immanent magic, purpose, and significance. Depression and ennui are not part of their lives. I can attest to this from personal experience: since doing philosophy became the mainstay of my life, the whole issue of meaning has disappeared, just as water disappears from the lives of fish. I am so immersed in immanent meaning that I don't think about it anymore. I do suffer—a lot even—but not because of a sense of meaninglessness or purposelessness. So although being a slave to the Daimon is often excruciatingly difficult, it does have this handsome payoff: the so-called meaning crisis that saddles the *Letzter Mensch* becomes so remote and abstract as to effectively vanish into thin air. This, too, is a telltale sign of Daimonic orientation.

The final sign of the Daimon's presence may only occur in extreme cases; so extreme, in fact, that one may refer to them as

Daimonic possessions. In such cases, the Daimonic orientation takes over one's life so completely, so thoroughly, that one can become cold and aloof towards the *personal*—such as relationships, friends, and family—for that is not the business of the Daimon; only the impersonal is. Steve Jobs's was just one such case, as was Kierkegaard's, who deliberately abandoned the love of his life—Regine Olsen—so to be able to focus entirely on his philosophy, despite thereby condemning himself to the pain of a broken heart for the rest of his short existence. People who are callously owned by their vision tend to behave callously themselves, thereby radiating the overwhelming and brutal presence of the Daimon within.

Daimonic possession represents one of nature's extremes and is arguably not necessary for the fulfillment of one's destiny. To guard against it, one must—again—always remember to maintain distance between one's ego and the movements of the impersonal within, so to be able to pass objective, balanced ethical judgment on the often-unreasonable demands of nature. After all, the meta-cognitive ego, too, is part of nature, and as such has a natural function to perform.

Our lives as Western minds aren't ours, but instead serve the Daimonic orientation within. Your life is not, has never been, and can never be about you, for the same reason that the life of an apple blossom obviously isn't about the apple blossom. *Your life is not about you*, and this should be obvious to anyone who thinks the question through. Yet, in the first half of life, the focus does lie on the ego's goals, because this is a necessary step for the development of an effective instrument of natural expression. In the second half, however, we must allow the impersonal force within to take over and play the instrument according to the Daimon's own holistic telos, which is incomprehensible to any human. Living in this natural manner eliminates all doubts about the presence of meaning in one's world, as life becomes saturated with it. It does require, though, a letting-go of the ego's agenda in the second half of life, and an embracement of nature's impersonal calling. It remains critical, nonetheless, to maintain the meta-cognitive ego's moral supervision of all Daimonic impulses rising from within, as the Daimon itself is an instinctive, spontaneous, "blind" —Schopenhauer's word— force of nature, akin to a volcano or tornado. It has unfathomable energy and can propel us to great heights but can also cause great destruction if left unsupervised.

Chapter 7

Prometheus's Sacrifice

In the Greek myth, Prometheus steals the fire of the gods from Mount Olympus and gives it to humanity. This is an act of self-sacrifice, as Zeus promptly punishes Prometheus by chaining him to a rock, where an eagle comes every day to eat his liver. But because Prometheus is immortal, his liver regenerates every night, just to be eaten again the next day. Prometheus thus endures eternal agony for his sacrificial service to humanity.

This theme of self-sacrifice for a higher, non-personal purpose is one of the most archetypal in Western life. Christianity—a Middle Eastern religion that spread like fire throughout the Western world for a reason—is itself centered on the ultimate sacrifice of Jesus, the Christ, for the sake of humanity. Something in us resonates profoundly with this, which is a more-than-subtle clue to how we are put together by nature. Our instinctive awe of sacrifice tells us something profound about ourselves: deep inside, we *know* that sacrifice not only is a part of the game of life, but *the most indispensable one*.

A sacrificial life lifts us off the banality of the personal and links us into a broader web of meaning far greater than our own little stories. Once in that web, one feels cradled and supported by invisible, archetypal forces. Rilke once spoke of it thus:

> The following realization rivals in its significance a religion: that once the background melody has been discovered one is no longer baffled in one's speech and obscure in one's decisions. There is a carefree security in the simple conviction that one is part of a melody, which means that one legitimately occupies a specific space and

has a specific duty towards a vast work where the least counts as much as the greatest.

(*Letters on Life*, edited and translated by Ulrich Baer, The Modern Library, 2005, page 14)

Hollis perhaps put it most explicitly:

To live the journey of the soul is to serve nature, to serve others and to serve that mystery of which we are the experiment. Then we will have incarnated the invisible, made luminous this short episode between two great mysteries [namely, birth and death].

(*Under Saturn's Shadow: The Wounding and Healing of Men*, Inner City Books, 1994, page 133)

Regrettably, at the present historical junction we aren't quite attuned to the archetypal template of sacrifice that is deeply embedded in us. The shallow, frivolous culture of the *Letzter Mensch* is a navel-gazing one, which always seeks the shortest, easiest path to some form of personal numbing and stupefaction. Under the ethos of such an egocentric and addiction-oriented culture, sacrifice serves no recognizable purpose and thus makes no sense.

But such an unnatural relationship with sacrifice is thought-born and culture-bound, not innate or instinctive. The archetypal templates always latent in us, simmering just below the surface, continue to resonate with the notion of service to a higher cause—even at great personal cost—for such a notion instantly restores meaning to our existence. After all, there is a strong sense in which, by sacrificing ourselves to a higher purpose that survives our own ephemeral existences, we achieve a form of eternal significance. Life becomes meaningful in a way that transcends the claustrophobic narrowness and pettiness of the merely personal. The power of living a sacrificial life thus remains immense in the Western mind, even if we, today, aren't quite attuned to it. Rediscovering it will mark our deliverance from the culture of the *Letzter Mensch*.

It took me years to explicitly realize this and, even then, life had to basically force-feed me the full power of the realization through a long and sometimes agonizing process. For as discussed earlier, my death at 34 wasn't an instantaneous event; everything in me resisted a departure from my tried-and-true life strategies. The change was slow and dragged on, progressing one small surrender at a time, until the unspeakable freedom of the sacrificial life—our birthright as Western minds—finally dawned.

The first thing I had to let go of, not long after my death, was my marriage. My relationship with my then-wife had been driven by the values and goals of the first half of life. We shared ambitions and motivated each other in that journey. But once the second half dawned upon us, with its entirely different mindset and perspectives, we both became disoriented, lost our alignment, and drifted apart. We resisted letting go and tried to "fix" things. But there was nothing to fix; there was nothing wrong. Life doesn't abide by the cultural recipe of the time—in our case, that marriages should last till death—or cater to our insecurities. Instead, it pushes ahead in a *natural* way, which often contradicts our narratives and culture-bound ideals. This is what happened to us. Our relationship had served its natural purpose well, and then there came a time when it had to make space for something new, something consistent with the new phase of life we were both embarking upon. That was all. And thus, my marriage was the first personal sacrifice of a long series, all for the sake of the impersonal that moves irresistibly within all of us.

But just as easily as it takes, life also gives, especially when doing so serves the teleological arch of the impersonal. We just need to pay attention to the doors it subtly opens for us, so opportunities don't pass us by. Nature cannot benefit from dysfunctional instruments, servants who can't do their job because they are lost, overwhelmed, or hopelessly unfulfilled. And so it was that someone else appeared in my life; someone completely, *utterly* different from both my ex-wife and my own intellectual ideal of what a partner should be like. Indeed, here was someone who had never really related to the ethos of the first half of life — i.e., ambition, status, power, the whole shebang; here was someone already born in the instinctive wisdom of a natural, spontaneous life driven by the impersonal — she would say "intuition," "feeling" — not the ego's machinations and stories. Her name was Claudia.

Although we connected quickly at an emotional level, the alienness of Claudia's way of being when compared to my life up until that moment was unsettling to me, because our narratives didn't seem to align at a conceptual level. She was 12 years younger and was living her life in a manner very different from how I had lived mine when I was her age. I couldn't square this circle in my inner chatter. "How can someone so different be right for me?" I'd ask myself rhetorically. "How can this ever work? She doesn't fit *my narrative*." Indeed she didn't; nature doesn't care much about our egoic narratives.

Fortunately for me, the voice of the Daimon would always tear my egoic nonsense apart: "You don't have to commit to anything, life is not a contract. This relationship *feels* good to you right now, yes? So keep on going, find out where this will lead, stay open and curious, stop overthinking and judging everything. What have you got to lose anyway? You already died, so what are you afraid of? Everything you thought was right and fulfilling has just collapsed under your feet — so much for your great ability to judge. So stop whining and accept what life is offering you now." And so I did.

This was my second sacrifice: the letting-go of *narrative-based judgments of world and others*, in the name of trusting the impersonal and going with the natural flow of life. To me, this was an *enormous* sacrifice, for it meant giving up the one personality trait—my ability to pass objective judgment on people and situations, and then plan my life accordingly in a very deliberate manner—that had kept me alive and functional after my father's death. It meant giving up on personal long-term goals in the name of what *feels* right as I go. For someone with my character at the time, this was like jumping into a dark abyss of unknown depth, based purely on... well, *faith*; faith in the Daimon, in the wisdom of nature. There is no greater leap of faith than to surrender one's judgment of the world, plus one's personal ideals, for the spontaneous guidance of the impersonal. I had to learn to trust something I couldn't even define.

And so it was that Claudia—the greatest of all possible gifts of my Daimon, given at the time of greatest need—became the foundation of my life, the rock against which I learned to lean. Without her calming, centering, and inspiring presence, the Bernardo Kastrup you know, and his work, would hardly exist. For while my first four philosophy books—although consistent with my later work and still reflecting my current thought correctly—were products of anguished and grasping attempts at making sense of life, from my fifth book onwards they were the expression of a calmer, self-assured inner certainty enabled by Claudia's feminine presence. *More Than Allegory*, in particular, was the wording of insights that came to me *through her presence*; through her spontaneous, sincere, radiating relationship with religion, which I had never had myself. Before her, religion to me was at best a poor, confusing, merely allegorical retelling of ideas that could be expressed in better, more direct and precise manner. It was she who taught me, simply by being who she is, that there is much more to myth than mere allegory.

Throughout all this, the Daimonic pressure exerted on me in the form of my health anxieties never let up. Yes, I had already surrendered my marriage, much of my way of being in the world, my mundane ambitions, and my adaptive proclivity for deliberate life planning; I had learned to trust intuition and accepted my Daimon's greatest gift. Nonetheless, I still needed anxiety to drive me down the Daimonic path, the path of philosophy. Without it, I almost certainly wouldn't have done the metaphysics work that kept on insinuating itself to me every waking—and sleeping—hour. I say this because I know that I insisted on finding some kind of compromise with the Daimon, so to preserve the remaining vestiges of my old life and comfort zone, particularly my career. Don't get me wrong: my career *progression* had already stopped due to my life's Daimonic reorientation, but I didn't want to let go of its *status quo*.

Regrettably—or perhaps not—that's not how nature works; or, at any rate, not how my Daimon works: it doesn't compromise, for it doesn't need to, just as a tsunami doesn't need to compromise with what is on its path. My insistence on performing a balancing act between old and new ways made me resist the natural flow of life; it stuck chewing gum on the strings of the violin, thereby reinforcing the need for constant Daimonic torment, without which I would easily have reverted to "the old dispensations, the old comforts, the old dependencies." Therefore, with one hand the Daimon served me unforgiving agony, relief from which would only be granted if I sat down to write. With the other, it made sure that I had the lifeline required to survive it all, in the form of Claudia. Looking back at those times, I am in awe of nature's merciless, brutal wisdom.

Years went by this way. My resistance was formidable, particularly with regards to my work. For my career was what defined me the most. I was good at what I did, didn't have much left to prove, and thus felt comfortable and reassured. I found peace with making no further career progress but didn't want to abandon what I had already achieved. I didn't want to have to start over again elsewhere, with all the uncertainty and risk that comes with a new beginning. My financial security was important to me as well. But most crucially of all, my work at ASML was largely the center of my social life, a surrogate family of sorts. Many of my colleagues were my friends, likeminded people whom I could effortlessly relate to and count on. They didn't regard me as a source of wisdom—which is very isolating and oppressing, as I shall discuss later—but as an equal. My company's President and CTO was also a somewhat distant but important mentor to me. I had already sacrificed so much; I didn't want to go all the way down the path of abdication. It just didn't seem fair.

But then again, the forces of nature aren't understanding or accommodating; and they surely know nothing about fairness. After a couple more years, I tried to manage my increasingly debilitating health anxieties by seeking professional help. At first, I did so informally, with a friend from the USA—an experienced therapist already close to retirement at the time— who took his personal time to talk things over with me online. He helped me hold it together during some of the worst periods, for which I shall always be grateful to him. After another couple of years, and following his advice, I sought a more formal and regular therapeutic relationship with a local psychologist, which had the benefit that we could speak in person and in Dutch. But because I already had quite some introspective insight into the dynamics of my predicament, there were no low-hanging therapeutic fruits to harvest. We persisted nonetheless, for this, too, was part of my pattern of resistance against the full and uncompromising reorientation demanded by my Daimon: I preferred "treatment" to further sacrifice.

Over the next two or three years, my therapist and I turned every rock over in my psychological landscape to try and find the root cause of my seeming self-torturing. He, of course, was coming at it from a more traditional perspective, which didn't entail anything remotely like objective Daimonic influences. From his vantage point, the loss of my father at the tender age of 12 was the glaring elephant in the room: it *must* have been the key causative factor underlying my distress. I wanted to believe that too, for a father complex that strong could not *not* be playing a role, I figured. Yet, every therapeutic avenue associated with this diagnosis failed. Incredibly, it turned out that the loss of my father, though certainly traumatic, wasn't the cause of my predicament, at least not in a *direct* way. And deep inside I, of course, knew this, for I was already well acquainted with the Daimonic within. I just hoped to be proven wrong, for that would rekindle my hope for a compromise with the Daimon.

This years-long attempt to compromise, which reflected a sustained pattern of resistance against fully re-orienting my life, led my Daimon to steadily turn up the volume of my anxieties as a way to force my hand. Nature is relentless: the more you resist it, the higher the price it exacts from you. My friends, despite having only outside access to my struggles, noticed my obstinacy against what even they could see was the natural new direction of my life: full-time philosophy. Even they understood that the entire world was conspiring to point me in that direction, and that only I seemed to be oblivious to it. Fred Matser was the first to recognize this, years before everybody else, and insisted that I should make the switch. My fate was clearer to him than it was to me; that's how blind attachment to the old dispensations makes us.

Despite my friends' urgings, I continued to resist. I was too focused on what I stood to lose, as opposed to the upside of serving nature in a spontaneous manner. Loss had been a big part of my childhood, and I didn't want to lose more than I already had; I clung to the remnants of my old life. With therapy failing and anxiety climbing to new heights, something had to give; and it eventually did, in a most bizarre manner.

For years I'd had to contend with what I now know to have been but a mild level of tinnitus: a ghost sound produced by one's inner ears, auditory nerves, or even brain. It's a constant sound that cannot be stopped; it stays with you day and night, and there is nothing modern medicine can do to cure it. The condition is a form of chronic torture. One can only be helped to accept it, not to get rid of it. Mine started in very mild form in my late 20s or early 30s, when I used to scuba-dive regularly. Pressure differentials impinging on the ears, during deeper dives, can lead to it. It then got a lot worse in the summer of 2012, following an ear infection that turned it into an exceedingly annoying and loud sound—akin to scratching a clean dish with a knife. It brought me to the edge of despair, but I resisted. I learned to live with it for another seven years, having at some point declared victory: I could stand it; it didn't defeat me; life couldn't take me down, whatever it brought on. These were the last remnants of the Hero archetype in me, heroically resisting change and seeking to reassert itself.

Then, in early 2019, I had my home's alarm system upgraded. The technician, however, forgot to remove the old siren affixed to a wall in my entrance hall. Instead of calling him back, I figured I could remove it myself. So I climbed a little ladder with a screwdriver in hand, and stood with my face right in front of it. As I turned the screws loose, I remembered that these things have a security feature: the siren goes off if one removes it from the wall without first putting the system in maintenance

110

mode, which I didn't know how to do. I knew full well that my ears were already damaged, and that, if that thing went off right in front of my face, the damage would become catastrophic and the tinnitus much, much worse. I knew that the siren was made to be unbearable to hear from anywhere within the house—so to drive intruders away—let alone from an arm's length away. All these thoughts came to me, in full clarity, before I removed the thing from the wall. Yet, somehow, *I still did it.*

The siren, of course, went off in my hands for about ten seconds before I managed to pull its batteries out. It was indescribably loud. My ears immediately started pulsating, as if they were being physically squeezed in and out. I started hearing all sounds as if I were a meter under water. Unsurprisingly, my cochlear cells had suffered catastrophic damage; so much so that my doctor felt it was pointless to measure the extent of the harm—such knowledge would only distress me further—since there was nothing he could do about it either way.

My tinnitus catapulted to flat-out unbearable levels, sounding now like two dentist's drills, one inside each ear. The resulting stereo effect placed the sound right in the center of my skull, destroying the boundaries between me and it—I became the tinnitus, and thus couldn't find a place for it outside myself. It's a condition that can drive anyone to sheer insanity. The unspeakably obnoxious sound was the last thing I heard before falling asleep, and the first thing I heard upon waking up; there was no off button. It even started getting regularly incorporated into my dreams, as my sleeping mind frantically sought to reconcile itself with its permanent presence. I couldn't sleep for more than two or three hours per night; and even then, in fits and starts. As a matter of fact, I'd rather describe it as passing out from exhaustion every night, instead of falling asleep. Because I was continuously—though subconsciously—contorting my facial muscles in response to the tinnitus—the way one cringes when hearing an annoying sound—I started getting cramps in my face and even jaw muscles (yes, such a thing really can happen, and it hurts). To say that tinnitus is a form of torture is a vast understatement. It is impossible to convey what it is like to live with severe forms of it, so I won't make further efforts to do so. It suffices to say that, in the Netherlands, severe tinnitus is legally considered a valid reason to request euthanasia—it constitutes "unbearable suffering with no prospect for improvement"—and there has been at least one publicized case of it.

I endlessly asked myself why, just *why* I had pulled that siren off the wall while knowing full well what the immediate consequences were going to be. I wasn't confused or cognitively impaired in any way whatsoever when I did it. I knew what I was doing. Later, I played the tape of the event back in my memory again and again, hundreds of times, compulsively trying to find how, just *how* this knowledge didn't stop me. I'm sure I wasn't covertly trying to punish myself—I can be self-deprecating, but not self-destructive. So there had to have been a moment of madness in those fateful few seconds, I reasoned. Yet, while playing the memory tape back, I could find no such moment. Indeed, I pulled that siren off the wall as calmly and deliberately as I am writing these words now, despite my full knowledge of what was going to happen next; it's incomprehensible. Of all the crazy moments in my life, this—and perhaps another one that is irrelevant to the subject of this book—made the least sense; I just couldn't wrap my head around it. I would never believe a story like this had it not happened to me. It was unreal, as if I were possessed.

And indeed, possessed I was: of course it wasn't me who pulled that siren off the wall; *it was the Daimon*. In the couple of seconds between my realizing what I was about to do to myself and the removal of the siren, the Daimon reflexively recognized a golden opportunity to achieve its goal. What goal, and how my harming myself would further it, would become clear to me only a couple of months later.

Over the weeks that followed, I repeatedly questioned my will to live. I did somehow manage, with great difficulty, to remain functional at work—which at that point was second nature to me—but even the small things in life, such as enjoying an evening movie or having a Sunday afternoon nap, became impossible. There was only *one* disconcerting exception to this rule: despite everything, *I could still do and write philosophy effortlessly.* As a matter of fact, I publicly defended my second PhD—in philosophy of mind—in April of 2019, during the peak of the torture. I also finished the manuscript of my book *Science Ideated* not long thereafter. That book was completed deep in the fires of hell, in my third visit to Hades. It is still nearly unbelievable to me that that was possible at all. My attitude while writing—a consolation of sorts—was that, if I could no longer live, I would at least get that last book out. This thought—similar to those that motivated the writing of most of my earlier books—allowed me to focus sharply on the task at hand, despite the torture. In a sense, getting the book finished was akin to getting permission to quit life.

Twice I seriously—*very* seriously—considered committing suicide, both times late at night, as Claudia lay asleep. At least once I got to the concrete planning stage, as someone with my background tends to know precisely how to end one's own life without drama, using items available in any home. I even started writing a goodbye note. For a period of half an hour or so, each time, suicide wasn't a remote, abstract possibility, but *something that was really going to happen shortly.* I reasoned that I had already lived a rich life, traveled the world multiple times, accomplished much, and that I had no need to keep on going like that; no, thank you very much, I already earned my Obol to pay the ferryman so it's time for me to check out. What stopped me was a mixture of (a) cowardice; (b) the knowledge of what Claudia would wake up to find the next morning, and how unfair that would have been to her; and (c) a subtle but sticky intuition that there was a hidden purpose behind the whole thing, and I just needed to wait a little longer to figure it out.

Something very defining changes deep within one when one has seriously contemplated suicide at least once, even if only for a brief moment; something that can never be reset afterwards: *one becomes incapable of making choices based on what one has got to lose,* for one remembers how ready one was to voluntarily lose *everything.* From that moment on, all choices can only be based on what one has yet to try or accomplish. This is the indelible mark that near-suicide permanently leaves in one's psyche. And it is exactly what the Daimon needed to do to me, because the reason for my years-long resistance against a complete reorientation of my life was precisely my fear of losing whatever I stood to lose, such as my career. This is why the Daimon pulled that siren off the wall.

So there I was, on the ground, finally beaten to a pulp, thoroughly defeated, comprehensively subjugated by life, by the Daimon, and ready to give up on everything. The Hero had lost the last fight and could no longer offer any resistance. How could I possibly worry, from that point on, about losing my financial security, social life, etc.? How bad could quitting my career be, when I had just been ready to quit my life? All my attachments became small, mere shadows on a cave wall. I had just been on the brink of surrendering *everything,* why would I hesitate to surrender shadows? Life is about what is yet to be tried, not what has already been accomplished; for at the end, we all walk out naked and empty-handed. When the betting stops, we can't take the chips with us anyway, so we might as well collect new experiences and form new memories instead, in service of something that transcends our personal selves.

In early June of that year, when I was still deep in the throes of despair, Fred came to visit. We sat at my dinner table, Fred in front of me and Claudia next to me. I told him everything about my struggles, in disturbing detail, as if trying to offload my pain onto the tabletop. He listened patiently. At some point, however, I fell silent, exhausted of reaffirming and amplifying my own suffering by repeatedly talking about it. After allowing for a brief, still pause, Fred then looked me straight in the eye and said: "I believe you still have a lot to give. Join me in starting a new foundation centered on philosophy and let us change the world for the better. I believe in you. Will you come with me? Tell me *now*." He sustained his firm gaze while awaiting my answer.

I was floored by those remarks. Consumed by my own self-commiseration as I was, the last thing I expected Fred to do was to give me a life-changing ultimatum like that. He had made similar proposals before, but under normal circumstances. At that particular moment, however, I was trying to survive, not thrive; trying to hold on, not start something anew. Yet, instead of reassuring me, he was asking me to jump into the unknown, at the very moment of my greatest vulnerability. In a sense that was insensitive, but something in me recognized it as Daimonic instead: Fred was serving as an instrument of my Daimon, inviting me to my destiny. "Calling crystallizes in that person whose face calls you to what feels like your fate," said Hillman (*The Soul's Code*, Bantam Books, 1996, page 144). Either way, Fred could see what I, without an outside push, couldn't. And he knew that too, so he pushed.

As I mentioned, Fred had proposed similar things to me before. Every time he did, however, my fear of abandoning my comfort zone—of losing my perceived career safety— made me effectively turn his offer down. This time, however, I experienced what was essentially the same proposal, from the same man, in a completely different way: suddenly it felt like a tiny dot of light at the end of a very long and dark tunnel, a fragile glimmer of hope, the inception of a new purpose, a new reason to remain alive. What I potentially stood to lose by accepting Fred's proposal was now irrelevant, abstract, hardly worth a thought. The Daimon had primed me for that new slant, that new way of experiencing the opportunity being offered to me via Fred. And the timing was critical: there was only a very short window of opportunity—a delicate balance between hopelessness and the remnants of my will to live—to catch me in just the right frame of mind. Through Fred, the Daimon scored the bull's eye in the center of that window. A day earlier or later, under slightly different conditions, I would have either insisted on holding on to my comfort zone or be past the point of caring about life. Looking back, I am again in awe of nature's brutal wisdom.

Still disoriented, the words of my answer slowly began to emerge from some place deep within me, and I could hardly believe them. I looked at Claudia and asked for her opinion. She knew that accepting such a change would mean a serious financial hit for both of us, not only in terms of my immediately losing my retention package and bonuses—which were substantial—but also in monthly income. Nonetheless, she nodded and told me that I should just follow my heart. I then turned to Fred and uttered—in disbelief—the words that had just come up: "Okay, let's do it." It was a decision unlike any other in my life; one I, exceptionally, made in the thick of emotional upheaval and based on intuition, instead of my usual, careful deliberation.

Right then and there, my transition from the first to the second half of life entered its final straight; the walls had been breached; the last bastion of the old dispensations—my professional life of 25 years—fell like Troy. I finally fully embraced the Daimonic orientation: philosophy was to be the core of my existence. This was the beginning of my sacrificial life—not because it would be painful, but because it was to serve an impersonal teleological arch, as opposed to my personal agenda. From that point on, I was to live in a manner fully informed by the knowledge that my life isn't about me; had never been and would never be. My life isn't about my personal goals, insecurities, ambitions, or tinnitus; it isn't even about my happiness. Instead, it's about the movements of the impersonal as it stirs within and without, in self and world. There is no place for self-commiseration under this ethos. My future—my hopes and expectations—was no longer to be set by my narrative self's machinations, but by the impersonal will of the Daimon. All I needed to do was to open myself up, every day, to the subtle but compelling sense of direction provided by it. Living life in this way means offering oneself to the call of the Daimon. This is the sacrifice. Soon I was going to finally become truly free: the absolute freedom of a life of total service. But not quite yet...

I wish I could tell you that, once it served its purpose, the tinnitus disappeared. Real life is a tad less romantic than that though. The tinnitus persisted and thus helping me deal with it became an extra challenge for my therapist. Acknowledging the failure of our efforts up to that point, he decided to change tack. His therapeutic intuition at that critical juncture was so refined that it, too, must have been covertly Daimonic.

And so it was that one day, somewhat out of the blue, my therapist asked: "Bernardo, what would you like to do *for yourself, for your own pleasure and gratification,* if you had the time, energy, and resources to do it?" This was the earth-shattering question that would reopen a long-forgotten door in my mind. But for the time being I didn't have an answer. There was *nothing* I'd have liked to do merely for my own pleasure. Since my death at 34, my entire life had been about *meaning*—Viktor Frankl's will-to-meaning having overwhelmed the Freudian will-to-pleasure in me—not about personal gratification. And for 22 years before that, it had been about *purpose*, not personal gratification. Even though I'd had fun times—Switzerland and CERN come to mind—I was completely alienated from the very idea of living *for* personal gratification; it wasn't a notion I could relate to anymore, for it had never been a part of my adult life. There was *nothing* I wanted for my own sake; nothing I really wanted to own, no place I really wanted to visit, nothing I really wanted to do merely for the pleasure of doing it. The Daimon had completely taken over my life, except for my residual— though persistent, tenacious—need to defend and preserve at least some of my comfort zone.

In hindsight, I understand now that the reason the Daimon had become so dominant in me was that I had lost myself and my personal dignity; I had lost touch with everything that defined *me* as an agent seeking gratification and self-fulfillment. My relationship with the Daimon was unbalanced because its presence obfuscated my very existence. What I had thought of as my fulfillment was in fact *its* fulfillment. Realizing this was the first step in holding my ground against the monstrosity of the impersonal in me. But I'm getting ahead of myself...

To my therapist, my inability to answer the simple question of what gives me personal gratification—not meaning, not purpose—was alarming, and he knew then that he was finally on to something. He insisted on having me think about it, despite my drawing a blank every time he asked the question. He instructed me to go back to a time *before* my father's death and remember what made me enthused and giddily happy as a child. Unbelievably, it would take months of this prodding for the obvious answer to finally come to me: I loved climbing mountains and tinkering with computers; these were the two passions that were *mine*, not the Daimon's; they defined *me* against the backdrop of the impersonal; they embodied my own personal dignity. And although I had never completely lost touch with the mountain part of the equation, the computer part had fallen by the wayside. Indeed, I had gone to computer engineering school—having just turned 17—precisely to build my own bespoke computer. Yet, since my professional life started in earnest, I had never done so. I had joined many large projects and teams, contributed to many complex systems as an engineer, but had never built my own computer from scratch, which was my original dream. Later in life, having transitioned from engineering to management, the dream was even forgotten. How cavalier of me; how insensitive towards the wide-eyed kid I once was; how cruel, even.

I had unknowingly sacrificed the child in me when I was just 12. This, in fact, had been my very first sacrificial act in life. But because it had been an *unknowing* one, it wasn't authentic and thus didn't count. I had killed little Bernardo for my own sake— little Bernardo was the one in pain, thus killing him would kill the pain—not for that of nature. Only a knowing, deliberate sacrifice counts when it comes to life's meaning, for one cannot harvest what arises from an unconscious act. Therefore, to truly sacrifice myself in the name of nature I first had to *be* myself again; I had to find myself first, so as to knowingly forgo myself. *This* was the indispensable act of deliberate volition that would at last seal my transition from the first to the second half of life. Following the example of the Christ, we must be able to say, in full consciousness, as the cross appears in the horizon: "may *Thou* will be done, not mine." *This* is the second great initiation to life. And to undergo it, we must first know *our* will.

My rapprochement with the dreams and desires of my child-self—the closing act of my years of therapy—played out in the first months of the COVID-19 pandemic, in early 2020, shortly after the production of my book *Science Ideated* was finished and no more inputs from me were required. Just as I rediscovered the simple enthusiasms of the kid still powerfully alive within me—namely, my old, unfulfilled love for designing my own bespoke computers—the lockdown forced me to spend almost all my time at home. There was something highly synchronistic about all that, as tinkering with computers became the obvious thing to do at home, to fill the void left open both by my forced social abstinence and the completion of my latest book.

I quickly set up a fully equipped electronics laboratory in my attic, and even invented a social media alter ego to go with it: *The Byte Attic*. There, in relaxed late-night hours, I started restoring old computers and designing brand new ones, from scratch, chronicling the whole thing in a kind of video diary of my lab activities. Music from the '70s and '80s always played in the background. I felt closer to both my child-self and my father, who had an electronics bench of his own, where I watched him build all kinds of gadgets. The smell of molten solder and the look of old-fashioned DIP chips—integrated circuits with through-hole terminals—brought back so many memories and feelings, an entire way of being I had completely forgotten. They also revealed to me how alive my child-self had remained within me all these years; how vibrant he still was, frozen in time and untouched by the ravages of the decades. I finally had a taste, once again, of truly being *myself*.

As this was unfolding, I was also in the process of closing out my work at ASML and setting up Essentia Foundation, the new focus of my life. These latter activities reflected my sacrifice, my now-unreserved commitment to the agenda of the impersonal, which my computer activities balanced out. Also, at around the same time, I was referred to a psychiatrist by my therapist, because I had serendipitously found an obscure Turkish research paper suggesting that amitriptyline—an old tricyclic antidepressant developed in the late '50s—could be effective in reducing the perceived volume of tinnitus at subclinical doses, and I wanted to try it out. I didn't hold out much hope, but the psychiatrist thought it was a harmless-enough experiment and thus gave me the drug.

To my surprise, after a couple of weeks it *did* reduce the volume of my tinnitus. I know it because I had measured the original level by playing white noise with my phone, through a headset, and checking what the minimum noise volume was that still masked the tinnitus. I did the same experiment after a couple of weeks using the drug and the volume necessary to mask the tinnitus had decreased to 1/3 or 1/4 of what it had originally been. Although the remaining level of tinnitus would likely still be terribly disturbing and upsetting to most people, to me it was like a holiday away from hell.

Amazingly, the drug also had other positive side-effects. I had suffered from irritable bowel syndrome for a couple of years at that point, and the drug alleviated its symptoms considerably. I could also think more clearly and in a more focused way, with less parallel thought-processes running all at the same time in my mind like before. And most importantly: *I could sleep with pleasure again*, a full 8 hours per night. The only negative side-effect was weight gain, but that was a small price to pay for the benefits.

I also believe—though experts may dispute the validity of this first-person account—that, despite my taking but a small, sub-clinical dose of amitriptyline, it did alleviate my anxiety symptoms. The change took longer to be perceptible than the reduction of tinnitus volume, and it was also more subtle, but to me it was quite clear too. What feeds one's anxiety levels are self-reinforcing loops of rumination. The drug seems to have made those loops less strong, and thus easier to break, thereby preventing the anxiety from escalating. Over the coming months, I would experience a marked reduction in my psychological distress, because of both the drug and my newly rediscovered relationship with the child in me.

Now, the thing is: *I would have never tried a psychoactive medication before developing severe tinnitus.* I knew too much about the approval process of more recent psychiatric drugs, such as SSRIs, and thus had considerable prejudice about their effectiveness and potential for long-term dependency. Until a condition as devastating as catastrophic tinnitus afflicted me, I'd have stayed safely away from all these drugs. Only sheer despair forced me to experiment with one. And the experiment showed that what Barfield understood to be the case for the entire physical world also applies to a humble little pill: behind its material appearance, too, there lies something of the same essence as us—i.e., something mental, experiential—which can thus interact with our inner life upon being absorbed, due to its kinship with it. Pills, too, are rich in meaning, just as the Western mind instinctively knows to be the case for all objects.

The otherwise incomprehensible Daimonic act of removing that siren from my wall had, therefore, not only finally forced the completion of my life's reorientation towards the Daimonic—i.e., the sacrifice of my career—but also led me to the very tools that would help me cope with the Daimon's coercion—tinnitus and anxiety—and even other conditions that were afflicting me. Moreover, that act led me to double-down on therapy—which wasn't progressing then—and ultimately find my personal identity again, reconnecting me with my younger self. None of this would have happened without the then incomprehensible siren event. As such, once again it becomes clear how impossible it is to judge nature's acts without the perspective of time, *sub specie aeternitatis*. The same Daimonic forces that brutally forced me to comply with the path of philosophy also gave me the tools to cope with their own brutally, remain effective as their instrument, and find myself again so to counterbalance their presence. Nature's wisdom is overwhelming to those with eyes to see it. To call it mere coincidence is downright preposterous.

True freedom had finally dawned upon my life: the freedom of a slave chained to the Daimon, who knowingly sacrifices his life for the sake of nature—God, if you prefer—and, in return, gets a chance to be himself. So much weight was lifted off my shoulders: no more responsibility for outcomes, for being happy, for deliberately figuring out where to go, etc. Life became so much lighter and bearable, almost easy-going. And yet the Daimonic meaning that had suffused it before was still there, intact.

My relationship with my Daimon turned from one based on domination, conflict, and resistance, into a balanced—dare I say, even harmonious—one based on dialogue and respect. I got the chance to be myself, to pursue my own gratification for a couple of hours every night, in exchange for fully reorienting my life in the Daimonic direction of philosophy—both my own philosophy and those of other kindred spirits, as promoted by Essentia Foundation. I wrote my previous book, *Analytic Idealism in a Nutshell*, under this ethos, and it has been the least painful writing experience of my life, next to the present one.

But make no mistake: if I abuse my opportunity to be myself and procrastinate in my service to the impersonal, I am given warning signs in various forms, including brief returns to anxiety. The difference is that I now know to recognize and heed these warnings before they escalate. In my mind, I apologize to the Daimon and reassure it that I will promptly get my act together, which I do. The present book is an outcome of precisely such an internal dynamic in me: due to my procrastination, it has come out months later than it should have; but it *has* come out.

I now live my life "as a painful and lovely day in the history of a great pregnancy," as Rilke put it (*Letters to a Young Poet*, Merchant Books, 2012, page 45). Through me and my peers, nature labors to seed something new into the world, and to harvest what emerges—as a result of sacrifice—out of it. My life is thus sacrificial, in that it is lived not for my sake, but for that of the impersonal, even though it is now lived under an ethos of respect for my personal dignity. What a relief this is; the overwhelmingly oppressive tyranny of the you-must-make-yourself-happy creed is all but gone. And paradoxically, it is precisely the thorough, sincere abandonment of the strife towards personal happiness that, ultimately, has made me content. As I write these words, I breathe contentment and meaning, for I know both that my life isn't about me and that I am playing my part towards whatever it *is* about.

I no longer deliberately plan my long-term future. When I was in the corporate world, a question I would regularly get from my human resources managers and coaches was: "Where do you want to be in five years?" At the time, this sounded like the most reasonable question imaginable; after all, I must know where I want to go in order to take the necessary steps to get there. But today, the question sounds exceedingly naïve to me, the result of a childish misunderstanding of how life and nature work—it constitutes an invitation to wrestle control from one's fate, which is as silly as it is profoundly unnatural. So now *I never ask myself anymore where I want to be in five years*, because it's not my call. I know that the direction will be shown to me, at every crossroads, by something infinitely wiser than me. I have surrendered egoic control over my inner compass, replacing it with implicit faith in the impersonal. I will go where life wants me to go—and of course, use my intellect to then plan my steps accordingly—not where *I* want to go. I no longer trust myself to pick a direction. This is how I now continue to integrate my future—my hopes and expectations—into my eternal present: with the *curiosity* of someone who hasn't chosen the destination but is trusted with navigating the terrain, so to pursue his nature-given fate.

I have used this word many times in this book: *fate*. It suggests some form of predestation, even predetermination, which, in turn, seems to contradict the notion that life is meaningful. For if our future is already predetermined—as opposed to being the outcome of our free-willed choices—and all that is left to do is to go through the motions, what's the point of it all?

This is a tricky question, because the words "fate," "destiny," and especially "free will," are so ill-defined. For instance, fate and destiny may entail but a general, preferential direction in life—a favored path—not the predetermination of every twist and turn in it. One may be fated to become a philosopher, but exactly how one expresses that fate may remain open. Also, most people think of free will as something that is neither determined (otherwise it wouldn't be free) nor random (otherwise it wouldn't be will). The problem is that every choice is either determined by something—such as our own tastes, preferences, and dispositions—or merely random, like the throw of a coin.

As Schopenhauer said, "Man can do what he wills but he cannot will what he wills" (*On the Freedom of the Will*, translated by Konstantin Kolenda, Basil Blackwell, 1985, page 54). We don't choose our preferences, tastes, or dispositions; we're born with them. Neither do we choose our fears, anxieties, or even our next thought. The archetypal templates that define us underly our choices. This doesn't contradict any coherent notion of free will, since it still allows for our choices to be determined *by us*; we are free to choose *as* we want, just not choose *what* we want. Our will, and therefore our choices, are determined by what we *are*. And we can't choose to be other than we are, any more than an amoeba can choose to be a cat, or Beethoven could choose to be Goethe. *We are the archetypes we embody*, and thus our choices and lives are archetypally determined.

But if so, you might ask, what is even the point of reading this little book? For here I am, overtly trying to help you accept your identity and fate as a Western mind. Yet, if all is archetypally determined, whether you will accept them or not is a foregone conclusion; you just need to go through the motions. Under this view, is there even any point to your reading this book?

The answer is: *of course there is*. Think of a computer: it is a completely deterministic system, this being the reason it is so reliable. If you run a given program on a given set of data, the results will be reliably the same every time you run the same program on the same data. Nothing is left to chance in a properly working computer. Yet, the computer is constituted of many Integrated Circuits, or ICs. Each IC receives certain inputs, processes them, and generates its outputs accordingly. These outputs are then sent to the next IC, which receives them at its inputs, processes them, and generates its own outputs accordingly. And so on. Each IC is fully deterministic and, thus, so is the computer as a whole. But each IC also can only produce its deterministic outputs if it receives, at its inputs, the equally deterministic outputs of the previous ICs in the chain. Should you remove any IC from the system, the latter will fail to perform its task and achieve its goal. As such, although the system remains deterministic, each of its parts must still play their respective role, indispensably. Determinism doesn't render the tasks of each part redundant; they must still do their job.

There is a very restricted sense, in the context of this admittedly precarious analogy, in which we are like ICs in the archetypally determined universe, segments of an integrated whole. Even though the system may be deterministic, we still need to play our parts; I still need to write this book and you read it, so my output—i.e., this book—can serve as your input and be processed by you, according to your archetypal dispositions, thereby leading to the choices and actions through which you will further influence the world. Should I fail to write my output, or you to read it, things would conceivably unfold very differently, like a broken computer. Determinism, therefore, does not contradict the meaning and purpose of any action, choice, or event in life; we must still play our parts, do our jobs, or the whole won't get to its ultimate teleological destination.

I don't mean by this precarious analogy that we are mere mechanisms; as a matter of fact, I don't think we are. I also don't think that the so-called "physical" world is causally closed. I do believe, though, with Barfield, that the "physical" world is a mere appearance—Schopenhauer would say "representation"— of a deeper reality. This latter, *real* world, which underlies all appearances, is indeed deterministic in my view—even if in a manner inconceivable to mere bipedal apes such as us—for the only alternative is fundamental randomness, a likely incoherent notion. It is in this spirit that I believe it important for us to see through the conceptual confusion that the notion of free will often rests upon, this being my motivation for using the analogy above.

There is an alternative but coherent conception of free will— which I've affirmed in my book *Why Materialism Is Baloney*— that isn't dichotomous with determinism. As my long-time readers know, I argue that the universe, at its most fundamental level, is a spatially-unbound field of subjectivity—i.e., one universal mind. All natural phenomena are but excitations— "vibrations"—of this field, as a musical note is an excitation of a guitar string. And since there is nothing in nature but the field—i.e., there is nobody playing the guitar—it must be *self-excitable*; it must have an inherent, endogenous impetus towards changing its own states. What we loosely refer to as "free will" *is this endogenous impetus*, which we experience directly, since we are segments of the field ourselves. As such, free will *does* exist, but it doesn't contradict determinism. On the contrary: free will *presupposes* it, as the impetus to self-excitation is a necessary expression of what the field *is*. In other words, the field does what it does because it is what it is; its actions are determined by its very being. Yet, its actions are still free, in the sense that they are determined by the field itself, not by any force external to the field—there is nothing outside the field.

The amazing journey of life is still magical, meaningful, astounding, even if, at its most fundamental level, reality is deterministic. For we know that the universe is computationally irreducible. In other words, we cannot calculate in advance, with full precision and based on microscopic first principles, where the universe is going. The only way to know is to wait for the universe to go through its motions and get there by itself. Relatively simple dynamics within the universe—such as the trajectory of an artillery shell or the movements of the moon—can be predicted in advance, through computational shortcuts and many simplifying assumptions; but *not* more complex subsystems such as the choices of a living being, let alone the precise future of the universe as a whole. To do so would require a computer larger and more complex than the universe itself.

Therefore, if the universe—as a mind or field of subjectivity—wants to know itself, it must go through its own motions, its own self-expression; there is no shortcut. There can be no advance knowledge that would render the motions redundant, so they are meaningful and necessary. If the universe is to eventually make sense of itself, it must observe its own unfolding through the eyes of living creatures such as you and me—in other words, *it must allow itself to happen*. Whether its motions are fundamentally determined or not is irrelevant in this context: *nothing* can know our future before we get there ourselves, because we are too complex for our choices to be anticipated. *Every choice we make is a moment of self-discovery, therein lies its meaning*: "oh, I am that which makes such a choice under these circumstances; how interesting." Every natural event is a moment of natural self-discovery at a universal level. So the journey is still one of great import and significance, determined or not. Life in the world is an epic, sacrificial research effort in the enterprise of natural self-discovery. The more we pay attention to life as teacher, the more successful the effort will be.

Allow me to belabor this point, for it is important: the computational irreducibility of the universe implies that determinism is *entirely irrelevant*—a mere theoretical abstraction—when it comes to the meaning of life. It just doesn't matter whether salient events are determined or not, since the only way to know where nature is going is to let it happen and observe it as it does. The only way for our choices to become known is for us to make them—God Itself cannot know them in advance. The only way for us to know our destiny is to live it, embody it. Only then does nature figure out what has always been latent in its own being, in archetypal form. And that is why living in full engagement with the world, deterministic as it ultimately may be, is profoundly meaningful for a Western mind.

To live a sacrificial life is the Western mind's great liberation, the only path to true meaning and sustainable contentment that is natural to us. It means being part of something so vast it is incomprehensible; something that survives our ephemeral lives, and through which we attain eternal significance. In our historical efforts to live according to the example of the Christ— the *Imitatio Christi*—we have given expression precisely to this archetypal template built deep into our minds and hearts. The crisis of meaning we have been living through since the late ninetenth century has to do with our having lost touch—because of the obfuscating influence of cultural narratives—with this ever-present inner reality.

Sooner or later, we are each bound to recognize the futility of our desperate attempts to attain mastery—complete control— over life and world. Upon reaching that liminal crossroads, we face a choice: either to double-down and try to usher in the *Übermensch* — as Nietzsche did and ultimately failed — or to surrender to the Daimon, lay our lives in the arms of nature, and be of service to the impersonal in us. Life — the great teacher, the only guru a Western mind will ever need — teaches the way of sacrifice to those who are willing and pay attention.

Chapter 8

Returning Home to Ithaca

Our siblings, the Eastern and Middle Eastern minds, have come to our rescue at multiple junctures in our history. When Rome fell and Western civilization regressed to a primitive state for a thousand years during the Middle Ages, it was Middle Eastern scholars who kept the torch of knowledge lit. In science, they developed chemistry (or "alchemy," as it was called at the time, from the Arabic "al-kīmiyā" or "الكيمياء"), algebra ("al-Jabr" or "الجبر"), the Arabic numerals we use today, observatories and astronomical tables, medicine, etc., much of which they gifted to us when we re-emerged from darkness during the Renaissance. In philosophy, Al-Farabi and Avicenna developed theories of logic, Ibn Arabi made profound advancements in metaphysics, and so on, while we were overwhelmed by superstition and, later, taken in by the empirical blindness of Scholasticism. Moreover, it was Arab scholars who preserved our own classical canon—the writings of the Greeks and Romans—and handed it back to us during the Renaissance, thereby preventing its permanent loss.

Much later, during the conceited insanity of Logical Positivism and Behaviorism in the mid-twentieth century, it was the philosophy of the East—Advaita Vedanta, Kashmiri Shaivism, Tibetan Buddhism, Daoism, Zen Buddhism, etc.— that kept us barely lucid, preventing a catastrophic descent into total nihilism. They informed the hippies, the human potential movement, our wellbeing industry, our psychology, and so on. Spiritually, they've kept us alive, for we have largely lost touch with our own spiritual path.

We have much more to thank the Eastern and Middle Eastern minds for than most of us would feel comfortable acknowledging. Having known this for much of my life, for years I've secretly entertained the fantasy of thinking of myself as a misplaced Eastern mind. Such a fabricated, wish-fulfilling self-image was further motivated by my shame for the great catastrophes imposed on life on Earth by the eager, Daimonic Western mind: colonialism, imperialism, slavery, forced conversions, the inquisition, the crusades, capitalist predation and exploitation, industrial pollution, the industrialization and commoditization of animal life and death, wars, etc. And when I started writing about philosophy, many recognized in my ideas—to my unabated delight—strong echoes of Advaita Vedanta, Kashmiri Shaivism, and other Eastern currents of thought. All this fueled my embarrassed, guilty, escapist ego's desire to identify with the wisdom of the East and renounce my Western heritage, a naïve delusion I would come to see through only in my 40s.

But before I elaborate on the insights associated with that turn of my life, allow me to make an important disclaimer: despite my overt admiration and respect for Eastern philosophy and psychology, I have never become an expert in either; as a matter of fact, I have never become even a decent student of the Eastern canon. So one should take what I am about to say below with a grain of salt. My views are informed by limited personal experience, as opposed to in-depth scholarship or field research. One could even say that they are merely my *impressions*, which I find adequate to share here just because this entire book is based on my own experiences anyway, as opposed to a work of objective, detached scholarship.

The Eastern mind embodies an admixture of archetypal dispositions very distinct from that of the West. There is no right or wrong here, just nature and its discernible differentiations. To characterize these differentiations, I must first illustrate them through concrete examples—in the hope that you will recognize them in your own experience—instead of jumping to broad and abstract generalizations. In this spirit, here are some of the examples that I personally find most striking.

Both the Eastern and Western minds have achieved the awareness that the so-called "physical" world—i.e., the contents of perception—is mere appearance, not the real world as it is in and of itself. The latter is concealed from us by the intermediation of perception, which merely *represents* the world, without *being* the world. This is analogous to how the states of the sky are concealed from an airplane's pilot by the intermediation of the airplane's dashboard, which also merely *represents* the sky, without *being* the sky.

In the East, perceptual appearances are often called the "Veil of Maya," illusion, as opposed to reality. In the West, different scholars have used different words to describe the same dichotomy: Owen Barfield talked of "appearances" versus "the unrepresented"; Henry Corbin of "symbols" versus "imagination"; Schopenhauer of "representations" versus "Will"; Immanuel Kant of "phenomena" versus "noumena"; Emanuel Swedenborg of "correspondences" versus "spirit"; Spinoza of *"natura naturata"* (also "modes") versus *"natura naturans"* (also "substance," "οὐσία"); my own friend Federico Faggin speaks of "icons" versus *"nousym"*; and even I have spoken of "extrinsic appearances" versus "intrinsic view."

The point here is that both the Eastern and the Western minds have had the same critical realization regarding the nature of reality. *But the respective ways in which they respond to this realization is radically different*, reflecting their respective archetypal dispositions. To the Eastern mind, the recognition that perception is a form of illusion tends to lead to *disengagement from the world*. The Eastern mind's commitment to truth is so complete and uncompromising that anything not regarded as true in and of itself fails to command its interest. Instead, the objective of the second half of life becomes an unmediated, direct relationship with truth, achieved by *abandoning the world of the senses* and focusing, instead, on pure introspection. In Tibetan Buddhism, this is encoded in the notion that the goal of life is to stop the "Wheel of Samsara," the cycle of successive reincarnations, so one no longer needs to come back to the world at all; in other words, *the goal of life in the world is to stop life in the world*! Such an active, uncompromising desire for disengagement is where the image of sages isolating themselves up remote mountains, to meditate alone for decades on end, comes from. They don't do that because they want to escape from their mundane problems, or to stop suffering by the grace of psychological sublimation or spiritual bypassing (it's Westerners that do it for these reasons); they do it because, archetypally, they just can't help but *not bother with what isn't true in and of itself.*

The Western mind's response to the same realization is almost the opposite: even if the world, as perceived, is illusory, such an illusion is itself still part of nature; it is something nature, for better or worse, is doing. For illusions exist as such: *as illusions*; they aren't nothing. The Western mind intuits that "behind" the illusions—behind the appearances, the phenomena, the representations, the "dashboard," the Veil of Maya—lies that which is represented or symbolized by the illusions. As such, *illusions still point to something real*—just as an airplane's dashboard tells us something real about the sky—and hence remain interesting. Illusions have *meaning* in that they represent something beyond themselves. And because the Western mind is overwhelmingly committed to meaning, it then seeks engagement with the illusions. The world becomes a book to be read, a message to be deciphered through interaction. This, in fact, is the root of the archetypal Western intuition that matter is magical in some sense: it represents, symbolizes, insinuates something beyond itself; something of the same nature as us. And because of it, we fall in love with matter like

Narcissus fell in love with his own reflection. We serve nature in the second half of life precisely *by engaging sacrificially with the world,* not disengaging from it. We seek to embed ourselves in the world, and to allow the world to embed itself in us, often at our own expense. This is not better or worse than the Eastern mind's proclivity to disengaging from the world in its search for unmediated truths; it's just different, expressing different archetypal dispositions immanent in the fabric of reality.

Another marked difference is in how the Eastern and Western minds relate to nature's archetypes. *That* they both seek such a relationship is universal: nature's telos is to know itself, while nature's very being is defined by its archetypes; therefore, to know itself nature must express and engage with its own archetypes. As such, it is no surprise that both Easterners and Westerners, as parts of nature, seek such an engagement. But *how* they pursue it is idiosyncratic to each.

The Eastern mind—with its penchant for direct access to truth—seeks the *purest, most idealized* archetypal manifestations, as distilled and expressed in *myths*; they don't fancy intermediaries or proxies, this being the reason why the Eastern mind doesn't bother much with recording history. Let's take the archetype of the King as an example to illustrate this point: for the Eastern mind, every historical king is just a poor echo of the *archetypal King*, which itself is already distilled and captured in a culture's rich mythology. So why bother with particular historical names, the dates of battles, the fates of individuals, and so on—all but imperfect echoes—when a direct relationship with the distilled archetype is achievable?

The much more empirically oriented Western mind, in turn, does not easily recognize immanent reality in the rarified narratives of myths. Despite our own rich mythology, we don't take myths as seriously as the Eastern mind does; we consider them interesting fictions, as opposed to idealized archetypal expressions. We are, therefore, largely incapable of having a direct relationship with the archetypes in their pure form. For us, it is the *empirical incarnations* of the archetypes that carry weight, reality, and true import. We need to know when and where Henry VIII lived, how many wives he had, what their names were, which ones were beheaded, the lurid details of what happened in his bedroom, for how long his chronic leg-wound festered, which battles he won, and even—if only we could— what his toilet really looked like. We try to record every detail, preserve every written letter, work of art and architecture, and generally consider history our sacred heritage.

This shouldn't come as a surprise, as we express our own archetypal dispositions through engagement with the empirical world. It's only natural, therefore, that we should want to preserve the complete record of these engagements. The underlying motivation here is identical to that of the Eastern mind—namely, to serve as instruments to nature's pursuit of its universal telos through engagement with the archetypes— but the manner in which we go about it is quite distinct. Again, there is no right or wrong here, just natural diversity.

Both the Eastern and Western minds have also understood that the ego—the seat of personal identity, the narrative self born on this or that date, who does this or that for a living, prefers this or that food, etc.—isn't who we really are; both have understood that our real nature far transcends the ego. But then again, they differ in how they respond to this insight. The Eastern mind seeks the *dissolution* of the ego through removal or denial of its contents: we aren't this, and we aren't that; we aren't our thoughts, or our emotions, or our history, etc. This can be achieved through disciplined introspection, such as meditation and self-inquiry.

The Western mind, in turn, achieves the experience of true identity by *addition*—i.e., by enriching our sense of self to a point where the ego becomes *diluted* in a much broader context. Instead of denying or removing pieces of what we ordinarily identify with, the Western mind *swells* our sense of self: not only are we our present ego, but also our past and future selves, plus our ancestors and descendants, our spiritual family, the world we are surrounded by and which—as per Barfield's recognition— is akin to us in essence, and finally the entire *Axis Mundi*, the entire universe. In this unfathomably broad context, the ego becomes so diluted as to remain only very mildly relevant. And then the *coup de grâce*: through *sacrifice* to the Daimon, we use the diluted ego as a mere tool for the accomplishment of the Daimon's agenda, not the ego's. At this point, we reach roughly the same destination as the Eastern mind: the *kenosis*—the emptying out—of the ego, not through dissolution, but dilution instead.

In yet another distinction that ultimately leads to the same result, the Eastern mind seeks its own completeness by removing itself from time, so to experience itself in the timeless domain of deep introspection. Indeed, outside time we haven't lost any part of ourselves to the past or are yet to express any part of ourselves in the future; instead, we're eternally complete. But the Western mind isn't naturally predisposed to deep introspection. Instead, we are empirically oriented, meaning that we tend to spread ourselves—thinly—across time. For us, the experience of completeness necessarily entails integrating both our past (the memories of all we have abandoned or been robbed of) and our future (our hopes, dreams, insecurities, and anxieties) in the eternal present. To be complete, we must acknowledge and honor the empirical existence of these dimensions we call "past" and "future"—whatever they may ultimately be—so to be able to gather and integrate the pieces of ourselves spread along the entire timeline. Once again, there is no right or wrong here, no better or worse; there's just diversity.

Perhaps the most consequential difference between the Eastern and Western minds, in regard to how we live our lives, is this: because the Easterners ultimately seek to disengage from the empirical world and pursue their telos through introspection, they need a guide—a guru—to show them the techniques. Our shared empirical reality—culture, education, serendipity, synchronicity, etc.—can offer no help to the Easterners, since it is precisely that which they are trying to disengage from.

To Westerners, however, life and world are the teacher. *Life teaches*, as I hope to have illustrated through the example of my own life, discussed at length in the foregoing. An uncompromisingly Western life requires no guru, for guidance is provided by the Daimon, which expresses itself equally within and without, in self and world. Lessons come in the form of will, serendipity, synchronicity, illness, symptom, doors that open and doors that close, success and failure, opportunity and crisis, invitation and rejection, reward and penance, and sometimes even the seemingly insensitive but Daimonic friend across the dinner table. Life shows the way to those who *pay attention*, and no better guide could be conceived of.

The only reason why many of us fail to heed the lessons of life is that, because of our culture-bound metaphysical prejudices, *we don't pay attention to it*; we take the world to be stupid, mechanical, and life to be random, arbitrary. We think that only microscopic organizing principles, which can be isolated and tested in the confines of a laboratory, can exist in nature; while macroscopic ones, which only kick in at high levels of complexity—such as a nervous system, a neighborhood, a society, and even the entire planet—may be influencing our lives and choices at all times, hidden from us by the opaque blanket of our unexamined assumptions. We see no wisdom or message in life's events because we are conditioned to thinking of them as dumb and perfunctory. And since both life and world are often unfair—which, sure enough, *they really are*, as fairness is a human concept, not an inherent value of nature—we rebel against and refuse to listen to them, thereby missing out on the unfathomable value of what they have to teach.

You may have noticed that, implied in the seemingly various differences between the Eastern and Western minds discussed above, there is the same "theme," the same "smell": in each case, the Western mind differs from the Eastern in more or less the same way. Running the risk of inaccuracy by inadequate generalization, the Eastern mind seems to favor directness and a more no-nonsense ethos, while the Western tends to approach life in a more dramatic—meant here literally, as in taking part in an epic drama or novel—and even poetic manner. This *one* general difference reflects two facets or sides of the same underlying teleological arch. In other words, both Eastern and Western minds pursue the same understanding, but from the perspective of opposite sides of the same coin.

The day I finally realized this was the day I consciously accepted and deliberately affirmed my own Western identity. *I am who I am*, as nature made me, and I now accept it unreservedly. I do not need to be an Eastern mind to serve truth and find meaning; the natural path of the Western mind gets us there too. *I am a Western mind*, committed to engaging with the empirical world, reading it as a book and expressing myself purposefully within it, integrating the entire arrow of time in my own self, and learning from *life itself* as my guru. Affirming this publicly, in writing, as I am doing right now, marks my return home to my own identity, as Odysseus to Ithaca. This public commitment to honoring my own inherent nature is profoundly liberating to me, which I only truly came to realize *right now*, as I write these words. *I am who I am; and I am a Western mind*. There; it has been said. May these words resonate far into the future, as an integral part of my legacy.

But disconnected from the natural Western path as most of us are—overwhelmed by the pathological culture of the *Letzter Mensch* in which we live—it is understandable that we should seek solace in what appears to be a tried-and-true way to reduce suffering: the Eastern path. I have felt such a temptation myself. Yet I invite you to ask yourself: are you seeking what is *true* or just trying to suffer less? In the former case, the Eastern path does indeed resonate with you. But in the latter, it will be a form of sublimation, of spiritual bypassing, which may anesthetize you for a while but will never truly feel natural and real to you. It will be an uphill battle, always difficult, forced, perhaps even frustrating. The Western path, in turn, though excruciatingly difficult sometimes, offers the potential for breakthroughs that will fill you with meaning and contentment to the point of bursting. You won't have to subdue any of your natural dispositions—such as engaging unreservedly with the world of the senses, pursuing a life of purpose, honoring your personal dignity and self-worth, embracing past and future, regarding matter as symbolically rich, learning from life, and basking in the profound freedom of sacrifice—but leverage them. *There is a Western path*, and it is your nature-given birthright and heritage.

Some are bound to look upon this book very critically. They will consider me supremely arrogant for assuming that my own life and dispositions are representative of the whole of the so-called Western mind and respective path. They will argue that classifying humanity into distinct categories of innate psychological dispositions is passé, outdated, and perhaps even pernicious, for it creates divisions. They may even hallucinate that this book tries to rank the Western mind above others, thereby promoting some form of Western neo-chauvinism.

Allow me to respond to these criticisms—which may be your own—already here. *Nothing* in this book is an attempt to engender the notion of a Western mind in my own image; historically and anthropologically speaking, there have always been discernible distinctions in psychological dispositions across different human groups, which have far preceded my existence. Moreover, my use of my own life in this book aims merely at evoking *recognition through example*, not at creating anything in my own image. Since I am unable to come up with detached, analytic-philosophical arguments for the subject matter of this book—after all, there are many salient facets of life and reality that cannot be corralled into logico-conceptual frameworks—*my life is all I have*. Indeed, before the rise of Analytic Philosophy in the Positivism-dominated Western world of the early twentieth century, *their lives were all philosophers had to do philosophy*. Back then, philosophy was first *lived*, and only then written. Today we call that mode of philosophizing "Continental Philosophy." But back then it was simply *philosophy*. Nietzsche:

> We philosophers ... are no thinking frogs, no objectifying and registering devices with frozen innards—we must constantly give birth to our thoughts out of our pain and maternally endow them with all that we have of blood, heart, fire, pleasure, passion, agony, conscience, fate, and disaster. Life—to us, that means constantly transforming all that we are into light and flame, and also all that wounds us ... Only great pain is the liberator of the spirit. (*The Gay Science*, translated by Walter Kaufmann, Vintage Books, 1974, section 318)

This is the spirit of this book. My return home to Ithaca is not only accounted for in its pages, but also symbolized by its very appearance in my life. *My Daimon is an ageless continental philosopher*, not an analytic one. It uses me and my modern education merely to reframe its insights in analytic language, as a concession to our current cultural ethos. Given the subject matter of my previous books, this concession has been very useful in practice and conducive to the Daimon's teleological arch. But the subject matter of the present book is very different; analytic arguments are useless to convey its message. Therefore, here my Daimon more freely expresses its continental dispositions, using *my life, my lived experience*—instead of my intellectual ability to weave neat analytic arguments—to make its case. It does so in the hope that you will recognize in yourself what I bore witness to in my own life. Should this fail for any of the points I raised, you owe it to yourself, for the sake of your intellectual honesty, to simply disregard the point. Yet, I am sure—because there is nothing special about me or my life—that many of you *will* recognize much of what I've tried to say, and thereby realize that you, too, are Western minds with a natural path—a fate—of your own.

To classify humanity into minds Eastern, Western, Middle Eastern, etc., is not an attempt to create divisions, but to recognize natural diversity and foster mutual understanding. To judge others based on *our* values and dispositions, as if they were universal, is a recipe for misjudgment, intolerance, disrespect, conflict, and ultimately catastrophe. Only the recognition of diversity can promote understanding, respect, and cooperation. Moreover, recognizing our *own* natural identity—realizing what we are and, just as importantly, what we are *not*—is critical to a life well-lived: a life of *self*-understanding, *self*-tolerance, and *self*-respect. Western minds that do not recognize themselves are liable to drifting into nihilism, despair, or pursue an Eastern path that, for them, will be mere narcosis.

Wherever diversity is found, chauvinism is a risk; for—deluded as it is—chauvinism constitutes an easy psychological shortcut to self-validation. Think of so-called "racial" chauvinism, for instance: it's much easier to think of yourself as worthy because of your skin color or genes alone—which you were born with, never had to work for, and nobody can ever take away from you—than your acts and accomplishments in life. The latter must be earned, are hard and always in play, while the former are free and secure from the get-go. No wonder, thus, that racism is so pervasive in a species that doesn't even have races.

Admittedly, the same chauvinistic games—rooted in covert insecurity—can play out when it comes to groupings based on innate psychological dispositions as well, not just skin color. In characterizing Westerness as something akin to the Jedi, I may have played right into it. But notice that the exact same analogy also applies to the Eastern and Middle Eastern minds, as well as to any other: they, too, are groupings based on shared values and a common way of life. Therefore, they, too, are like the Jedi.

My challenge here has been to find a way to encourage you to recognize and validate your own inborn identity, and even be proud of it—for there is nothing wrong with being proud of who we are—without encouraging the hallucination that such self-validation implies inherent superiority or social/geopolitical entitlement; *it does not,* and I hope the foregoing—with its repeated acknowledgements of the many historical mistakes of the Western mind, as well as the many instances in which the Eastern and Middle Eastern minds have come to our rescue—has been clear enough in this regard. Nonetheless, notice that I cannot—no author can—make *absolutely* sure that my message won't be misinterpreted or misused by those determined to do so; all I can do is to be explicit and unambiguous regarding my position: *the recognition of our Westerness does not imply inherent superiority or social/geopolitical entitlement;* it is, first and foremost, about how we relate to *ourselves.*

Without a sense of identity—of belonging innately in something larger than us—we cannot find context and, therefore, purpose or meaning in our lives; we become a blank sheet floating aimlessly in the wind, without a past or a future, pushed around by the banality of mere circumstance, with nowhere to go. Our individuality as Western minds does not contradict the importance of our belonging in a broader context of kindred spirits. Unique as each of us is, we still have a family, a role in a bigger, collective play, and an overarching, shared purpose to achieve.

The freedom of surrendering the reins of one's life to the Daimon can only be felt, not described. I am still getting used to it, even though it has already been quite a ride; a poignant one, with very high ups and agonizingly deep downs, but always suffused with meaning. The nuances of a Daimonic life are still being revealed to me as I go. I sense what is coming: some of it is wonderful, exhilarating; but some of it is also cruel beyond belief, sending a chill of both anxiety and resentment down my spine. One's relationship with one's Daimon is emotionally charged, often acrimonious, and certainly not always understanding. One romanticizes the Daimonic at one's own peril.

It is impossible to really know the Daimonic trajectory of one's life in advance; it only truly reveals itself as it unfolds. The directions chosen by the Daimon aren't constants; they change so to adapt to circumstances, go round the buoys, tick the boxes, avoid obstacles, and leverage opportunities. Often, they zigzag. Nonetheless, as I suggested above, sometimes we *can* get a general sense of where it is all ultimately going; we can discern the blurry, vague outline of what is coming as it rises against the shimmering background of the far horizon.

In my case, what I fear to discern in the distance is something so cruelly ironic, so made-to-order to aggrieve me, that a big part of me thinks it can only be a bad joke. For what I think to see, far away, are the emerging contours of my last role in life: perhaps that of embodying the Old Wise Man archetype. This may sound romantic, perhaps even flattering; and goodness knows many out there expect precisely this from me, for they project onto me their own inner wisdom. Yet to me, this is a fate bitter beyond comprehension, for I am still a 12-year-old boy who lost his father. For most of my life, I have implicitly sought someone, *something*, to play the role of the Old Wise Man towards me; the role my father once played. This has been my greatest want, the gaping wound in my heart. Therefore, even though I've come to accept that the wound will never heal, that nature may expect—of all people—*me* to play that role is the ultimate betrayal. Only the old wise man doesn't get to have an old wise man to reassure him, so he is condemned to having a basic human need forever unfulfilled; *precisely* the need exacerbated in me because of what nature did to me as a kid. This is sarcastic cruelty dressed in almost sadistic irony. Expecting me to play this role is like charging the starving bum with passing food around to the guests of a cocktail party. It also kicks me upstairs, exiles me from the warmth of mutual human reassurance, and insulates me from redemption. It is a life-sentence in solitary confinement. To task this 12-year-old kid with finding his father *in himself* is deeply unfair, and I resent it with every fiber of my being. My confessing to this here is the only resistance I can offer, a form of protest committed to the record. Beyond that, I know there's just nothing I can do about it; after all, my life—just like those of all Western minds—is sacrificial. If a vessel for the myriad projections of others I must ultimately become, then so be it; may nature's will be done. Or perhaps mercy will take this particular chalice away from me; who knows?

What is clearer, because it is already very close, is the next turn in my path—luckily a more cheerful one. The process of writing this book has shown me that it marks an end and a new beginning, a turning point, an unexpected transition. From my thirty-fifth year till now, the Daimonic orientation has forced me to sacrifice what gratifies me, as an individual, for the sake of the impersonal. This has been my life as a professional philosopher, a role the kid in me never desired to play. But the twists and turns of the world—think of the emergence of Artificial Intelligence and how it is making of metaphysics in general, and philosophy of mind in particular, a mainstream topic—may be offering my Daimon an opportunity: that of leveraging the skills I have developed for my own gratification towards nature's telos. This—if it materializes—will be a rare but fortuitous alignment, in which doing what gratifies me happens to be precisely what is most conducive to fulfilling my fate. I await it with a small smile, while dreading, deeper within me, what may come later.

But these are chapters of my story—my fate—yet to be written by life and, of course, death. May this little book help you pursue your own, the story of your fate.

Framespotting

Changing how you look at things changes how you see them

Laurence & Alison Matthews

A punchy, upbeat guide to framespotting. Spot deceptions
and hidden assumptions; swap growth for growing up.
See and be free.

Paperback: 978-1-78279-689-3 ebook: 978-1-78279-822-4

Is There an Afterlife?

David Fontana

Is there an Afterlife? If so what is it like? How do
Western ideas of the afterlife compare with Eastern?
David Fontana presents the historical and contemporary
evidence for survival of physical death.

Paperback: 978-1-90381-690-5

Nothing Matters

a book about nothing

Ronald Green

Thinking about Nothing opens the world to
everything by illuminating new angles to old problems
and stimulating new ways of thinking.

Paperback: 978-1-84694-707-0 ebook: 978-1-78099-016-3

Panpsychism

The Philosophy of the Sensuous Cosmos

Peter Ells

Are free will and mind chimeras? This book, anti-
materialistic but respecting science, answers: No!
Mind is foundational to all existence.

Paperback: 978-1-84694-505-2 ebook: 978-1-78099-018-7

Punk Science

Inside the Mind of God

Manjir Samanta-Laughton

Many have experienced unexplainable phenomena; God,
psychic abilities, extraordinary healing and angelic encounters.
Can cutting-edge science actually explain phenomena
previously thought of as 'paranormal'?

Paperback: 978-1-90504-793-2

The Vagabond Spirit of Poetry

Edward Clarke

Spend time with the wisest poets of the modern age and
of the past, and let Edward Clarke remind you of the
importance of poetry in our industrialized world.

Paperback: 978-1-78279-370-0 ebook: 978-1-78279-369-4

Readers of ebooks can buy or view any of these bestsellers by
clicking on the live link in the title. Most titles are published in
paperback and as an ebook. Paperbacks are available in traditional
bookshops. Both print and ebook formats are available online.
Find more titles and sign up to our readers' newsletter at
www.collectiveinkbooks.com/non-fiction
Follow us on Facebook at
www.facebook.com/CINonFiction